GRACE NOTES

GRACE NOTES

Variations on a Greek Theme

NEIL MACVICAR

MICHAEL RUSSELL

© Neil Macvicar 1995

First published in Great Britain 1995
by Michael Russell (Publishing) Ltd
Wilby Hall, Wilby, Norwich NR16 2JP

Typeset in Bembo
by The Typesetting Bureau
Wimborne, Dorset
Printed and bound in Great Britain
by Biddles Ltd, Guildford and King's Lynn

Contents

I

Sunday, 10 June 1990

Today before breakfast I walked for the last time from the house in Samara Street to the hilltop above Old Psychiko. Tomorrow the removal men will begin to pack up Ina's furniture, the Giallina picture, the musk-rose tea-set, great-grandmamma Loukia from Odessa's silver samovar, and the fading sepia photographs of gentlemen in bowlers and high stiff collars and the ladies in huge flowered hats and long skirts, and all the other reminders of the past, and the next day the diaspora will start, some of it to Stevie and us in Corfu, some to Christine at Versailles, the rest to Elisabeth's new flat in Athens, as if Ina herself were being divided among her descendants.

For both Marily and me it is the end of roughly half a century's association with Psychiko. Round the corner, in Solomou Street, the house still stands where she lived through the war and the German occupation, with her mother and the twins, and Ina's second husband Pericles, and the baby Elisabeth and Koko the fox terrier and Josette the goat and a floating population of billeted Wehrmacht soldiers. There, too, I was entertained when I first got to know the family and, unsuspected, it was all beginning for the two of us.

I set off up that same street (named after Dionysios Solomos, the poet of the Ionian) which is still a proper old-style Psychiko road, of unpretentious houses, out of which unpretentious people emerge to wait on the pavement for the No. 603 bus to take them into Athens. At its lower end it has a tree-shaded rondpoint of a *plateia* with two newspaper kiosks (once on a time there was a café as well, but that was before the citizens lost the use of their legs from too much motoring), and at the top there is a smaller square with a bijou park and a single kiosk. The second half of the climb is up the length of Karkavitsa, which is the new-style Psychiko of enormous, and enormously expensive, apartment blocks, among which the only living things to be seen on foot are the domestic guard dogs, and the rhythmic swish of the lawn-sprinklers sounds like the rustle of banknotes being counted. Half way up there is a vast garden whose trees conceal a house where the Saudi Arabian ambassador is deemed to have his residence, protected from the human race by a fence of spears with gilded points, and a gate of similar construction decorated with golden scimitars and palm trees. On one side of this a security man sits day and night, and on the other two bullet-proof limousines await the royal Saudi command.

The sun was still low enough to keep the streets in shade, but the poplars threw a luminous green canopy over Karkavitsa, out of which I stepped, with the usual shock of pleasure, on to the saddle of the ridge, and another world. An open valley slopes steeply to the west, bare except for a low scrub of thyme and throumbi and dwarf gorse, precariously preserved from the property developers. Gipsies often camp in the valley bottom, their lovely, grubby children playing amid a shambles of big tents, scrap metal, garishly painted lorries, and lean horses. Today – a bad omen perhaps for conservation – the encampment had gone, but a shepherd and his three dogs were moving a large flock down the hill, and rows of blue and white beehives were still dotted about the slope.

The ridge is the northern extension of the Tourkovounia, the Turkish Hills (or what is left of them), the low range at the foot of which Psychiko was built, where Marily and Daisy and their other school friends used to climb on summer evenings to flirt and discuss life and art, and hatch dastardly plots against the alien occupiers. After the war the Athenian building boom got under way and the quarry on the hill worked around the clock, year after year, till the comely range had been eaten away into a vast mouth surrounded by a few stumps of rotten giant teeth. I turned the other way and walked to the bluff at the very end of the ridge, high above the Olympic football stadium. The ruined Tourkovounia block the view of central Athens, but to the right there is a blue glimpse of Salamis Bay, and then a clockwise panorama of the circle of mountains – Parnis, Pendeli and Hymettus – enclosing the monstrous sprawl of the capital.

At the very top of the bluff, near a surveyor's bench-mark, an elliptical jumble of stones proclaims itself, on a plaque, to be a sanctuary of Zeus, with the remains of an altar and the plinth for the god's statue. Over the years it has become, in its quiet way and, perhaps because no guide book mentions it, one of my favourite classical sites. Zeus's temples tend to be too big for my taste in religious buildings – the size of the scattered column drums at Olympia lead me to congratulate Poseidon the Earth-shaker on having cast down the house of the father of the Gods. Here the whole enclosure measures only some ten by fifteen paces, and reminds me of the vestiges of St Ninian's little chapel on the island of Bute, looking from its lonely promontory across the firth to Arran. Both are humble places of communion with heaven which have drawn men and women to make the effort of pilgrimage.

Marily and I brought Daisy here last autumn. She had come through her operation, and we picked yellow Sternbergia crocuses and talked hopefully of holidaying again on Andros, but the shadow of death already lay across her path. The cancer wasted her away and ate out her life even before old Ina died. We have little reason for coming to Athens now that we have lost our true, clever, funny, unlucky friend.

The house in Samara Street, too, is sad. These last years Ina was too sick and crippled to care for it properly. It became a prison in which she crept between her bed and the television set and the kitchen chair where she directed cooking operations, gradually losing interest in the world outside. Even the garden she had loved was becoming a half-neglected jungle.

In spite of such melancholy reflections, good memories outweighed the bad, on my hilltop among the swooping swallows. It was turning into one of those clear hot mornings that I remember from the Athens of forty-five years ago, when I fell in love in and with Greece. I thought of those days, and of all the sweet times Marily and I have had together, and the trips we used to make with Daisy in Italy and Scotland, as well as in Greece. I thought of Ina in her great days, building the Samara house at the time of her impulsive and ill-conceived third marriage, planting her fig and cypress and lemon trees, writing to friends all over the world, knitting for grandchildren, incessantly on the telephone, planning meals, eating too much, bossing her team of devoted daily women, organising all our lives, dominating every conversation and sallying forth to brighten the length and breadth of Europe with her big, buoyant ebullience. The letters we have received since her death tell the story.

So I came down, and when Marily and I had drunk our coffee we walked to Ay. Dimitri. The Liturgy was at its end, and Pater Efthymios, who was Ina's parish priest and had called her the Despoina of Psychiko at her funeral, was preaching with fervour about fighting the good fight. We lit candles for the living and the dead. The deacon came out with the chalice of the Sacrament, and several newly christened babies, clean and innocent in their baptismal outfits, were carried up to receive their first communion, and we all followed to take our *antidoron* of bread from Papa Efthymios's hand.

In all the large congregation we did not see a single face we knew. It was the end of the chapter.

2

Athenian Easter

The deaths, in the spring, of Marily's mother and of our dearest Greek friend, in such quick succession, made the whole of 1990 a melancholy contrast to the previous year. Then we had been celebrating forty years of marriage, and our new Corfu garden had rewarded us with lavender and roses and white and scarlet hibiscus. All our grandchildren had been there together with us, and had made friends with a troop of Franco-Greek cousins. Many of our own friends had visited us, and we had still found time to explore many facets of the Hellenic world, in both space and time.

For hors d'oeuvre there were a few days in Bonn, where Marily's sister Elisabeth, recently established with her new husband, was celebrating her fiftieth birthday. For both of us it was the first experience of Germany. The weather was cold and misty, the hospitality warm and lavish, and the Rhine magnificent. Bonn itself was marking the bi-millenary of the frontier station of Castra Bonnensia where a legionary looking across the wide river had at his back an empire which reached to Nile and Euphrates.

We left Germany under a lowering sky. The air-bus ground its way over a monotonous cloud-fleece that hid all the lands of the Teutons and Slavs. Then, all at once, the Olympians rolled it back and our flight-path was slicing the neck of Chalcidice's Cassandra peninsula. Ahead in a dazzle of light the Sporades floated with white necklaces of foam round their jagged rims. The plane crossed Euboea and Boeotia, made a long loop round Aegina, and began its decline athwart the shipping lanes of the Saronic.

It was Great Wednesday – the Wednesday in the Great Week, Meghali Vdomadha, that culminates in the Feast of the Resurrection. Easter fell late that year, at the very end of April. The next morning, while Marily went into town, I walked through the familiar Psychiko roads. Every garden was ablaze with roses in full bloom, some hanging over and perfuming the pavements. The orange trees had both flower and fruit, drowning all scents nearby. Ina's own tree was hung with lemons, and night-scented jasmine poured over the verandah. Here and there among the extravagances of Athenian suburban architecture a few vacant lots survived, sprinkled with ancient rubbish and a spectrum of wild flowers, from the purple and pink of mallow, rock-rose and convolvulus, through yellow phlomis and orange marigolds, to the small poppies' blood red.

I passed the church of St Demetrius and the stalls of the open-air market, passed into the shade of a low pine grove, and then climbed to a row of poultry-ridden cottages. Here the roadways petered out and the white rocks and the scrub began, of what was left of the Tourkovounia hills. None of it bore any resemblance to the regimented gentility of Bonn's front gardens. Marily told me on her return that Athens had filled her with the same feeling of relief – voluble crowds, street sellers of *koulouri* rolls, pavement stalls of bric-a-brac, the heat and sunlight of our Hellas.

It was only the second Easter we had spent together in Athens. The first had been thirty-five years before, when Katherine was three and Amanda a babe in arms, and we brought the children to be admired by their great-grandmother and all the family. We stayed then with Ina in a house she had rented at Nea Smyrni, between the city and the Phaliron shore. It was thought rather odd in a prime minster's granddaughter to be living among survivors of the 1922 Asia Minor debacle, rather than in the inbred, they're-cousins-of-mine-you-know, enclave of Kolonaki. The reason was that Marily's mother, defying all well-meant prophecies of disaster, was about to take the plunge into that improbable third marriage and was taking cover, out of range of her family and friends' sniping. Meanwhile she supervised the building of a new house in Psychiko. This, as things turned out, was not a matrimonial home for long, but was to be hers for the rest of her life.

I was not troubled by the social nuances. In fact, I was pleased to be back in Nea Smyrni, the first district of Greece that I ever knew. The place revived some of my more unusual memories: a bitter Christmas Day, celebrated with bully beef and hard tack, with 25-pounder guns barking among the flower-beds and yards, Mavrodaphni wine and the singing of 'Tipperary' at Mr Frantzis's multinational, all-ranks New Year's Eve party; the Carnival festivity at Mr Stamboulides' house which ended with death in fancy dress, and the funeral of our host. The untidy little suburb had been the school where I learned that the thing most to be expected in Greece was the unexpected.

My recollections of the return to Nea Smyrni nine years later were fewer and less distinct. My overall memory was that the spring days grew steadily colder as Easter approached, and that Easter Day felt more like Christmas. On the Sunday, Pericles, Elisabeth's father, offered to drive her and me to Delphi. The intention was to lunch at Arachova, above Delphi, where Pericles painted a mouth-watering picture of lambs roasting on the twirling spits. Of course we left two hours too late, and finished by standing in a snowstorm chewing scraps of tepid innards, while at Delphi dusk was threatening before we had time to visit more than the stadium. Yet that made up for the discomfort. The runners' starting-blocks and the empty tiers of seating are always evocative, but never more memorable than when the track is white with snow, pricked out with the spear-points of scarlet tulips.

And now, reminiscences and all, we were back for our second Easter, at the house in Samara Street. Ina was not well enough to travel to Corfu, and we suspected that there might not be another Easter for us all to celebrate together. It was not an easy visit. Pain and the frustrations of old age made my mother-in-law fractious. But we were able to observe the rituals of the season, and spent much time on the road between the house and St Demetrius. On Thursday evening we listened to the long reading of the Passion and were moved, as always, by the hymn sung by the priest as he carries the Crucifix round the church – 'Today is hung upon wood He who hung the earth in the waters...' On Good Friday morning the Epitaphion, Christ's funeral bier, was decked with red carnations to receive the crucified image, and after dark we followed its procession through the streets. A slow drum-beat went before, and the church ringers tolled the accompaniment of God's passing bell. The whole throng carried candles, the flames showing up, from below, the strong bone structure of alert, good-humoured Greek faces.

[From my journal:]
Great Saturday, 29 April Woke at 5 to a great clatter of bells from the early Litouryia at Ay. Dimitri. The first blackbird sang at 5.55. Got up at 7.30 to find all the clouds gone. We walked to church at 8.30 in rose-scented sunshine. They were singing the Song of the Three Children when we got in. Then the Epistle, and we were preparing ourselves for the Gospel (and a long haul through the Liturgy) when a priest appeared at the doors with the chalice and we had to scurry up to take communion, while the bells set up a great jangle, and Papa Efthymios, broadly beaming, threw bay leaves over everyone. Cheerfulness having broken in and our object being achieved, if rather breathlessly, we saw no point in waiting for a second Consecration, but came home to break our fast.

Walked down to the Pharos with M. She had her hair washed, and I bought one bottle of ouzo, one of retsina and one of red Naoussa Boutari – total cost c. 3.50.

We ate the right food at the right times – for lunch on Good Friday lentil soup with the addition of vinegar, black olives and boiled potatoes, and undressed lettuce and cucumber on the side, followed by halva and oranges; and after the Anastasi at midnight on Saturday (in a wind which made it hard to keep one's candles alight all the way home) *mayiritsa* soup made from lamb's lights, and hard-boiled red eggs, washed down with retsina. Sunday lunch was a traditional feast: a *meze* of aubergine salad with ouzo, more *mayiritsa* and red eggs, roast lamb and potatoes with a green salad, and a sweet of *galatoboureko*. (I noted that my journal was beginning to read like Parson Woodforde's diary, but it is difficult to avoid the topic of food in a land where its association with all the year's commemorations, both solemn and joyful, gives it an almost religious significance.)

The stimulus of organising a meal worthy of her reputation remarkably restored Ina's good humour. Daisy came specially from Porto Rafti to join us for lunch, and we all sat on the terrace shaded by the laden lemon tree and by the now towering cypress which Ina had planted in Amanda's honour when the garden first began. Daisy was having tests for some trouble on her lung. But she was her old self, smoking as many cigarettes as ever and amusing us with unsentimental comments on the behaviour of old friends and the artistic world of Athens. We left for Corfu two days later, and did not see her again till after her operation.

3

The People

Costa Botsi, who met us and drove us to Kapoutsi, was a retired taxi driver, with a hereditary status as most favoured chauffeur. His father Spiro, who came from our village, used to own one of the town fleet of vintage taxis which in the immediate post-war years, apart from the equally antique buses, constituted Corfu's only passenger vehicles. It was Spiro who had conveyed Marily and me on our first married journey. After the wedding reception he drove us through the darkness to begin our honeymoon at the Manessi house of San Stefano, with a halt at the village to buy a bottle of connubial ouzo. Costa had inherited the paternal taxi, and its permit, drove it and more modern successors for many years, and finally sold both at a price that enabled him to enjoy a prosperous early retirement. He earned extra, unofficial, income by driving former clients like ourselves. He also became my adviser on matters mechanical, and we were very fond of him and his wife Inez, a handsome woman who sang contralto in the municipal choir.

The spring drought had ended on the eve of Easter, in a cataclysm of rain which turned roads into rivers, and washed out both the Anastasis ceremonies on the Esplanade, and the alfresco roasting of lambs all over the island. We came up through sunshine to the village, but there were signs of still more recent rain and the countryside looked and smelled clean. The new roses and wistaria had begun to creep over the gateway, and the file of bitter orange trees along the drive were clearly passing from childhood to adolescence.

As we had hoped, old Olga had hung yesterday's May

wreath on our front door, and as we got out of the car she came round the corner of the house, leading Hussein the donkey. He quickened his pace and nuzzled us with his long hard nose, like a great grey dog. Greetings and embraces over, we opened up and went into an interior filled, by Irene, with spring flowers. All that the sleeping house needed was to be given the prince's kiss, and to be opened to its terrace, and the rolling landscape of olive and cypress, and the panorama of hills, from the Ten Saints to Pantocratora and the jagged profile of the Albanian mountains.

Olga and Irene complemented one another in helping us to run Kapoutsi. Olga, who was over seventy, had always lived in the village. She had been a sprightly girl, loving to 'climb up the olive trees and sing like a bird', and finally eloping with a handsome fisherman called Costa. The love-match produced one son (Niko the village blacksmith) and seven daughters, but was dogged by poverty because of Costa's drinking habits. By the time we first knew them the children were all married and away, and on bad terms with their father. Olga lived in a wretched house, not far from ours, alone with her old, bad-tempered, alcholic wreck, whom she tended uncomplainingly and referred to as her 'flower', her 'rosebud'.

Hussein had been the origin of his mistress's entry into our life. Olga had been accustomed to tether him on our land's rough pasture, before we acquired Kapoutsi. We did not mind if this continued, and agreed that she might use our *litrouvio* – the former olive press by the gate – as a stable. In return Hussein provided us with manure, and Olga did odd jobs in the house. She worked in her own time, giving priority to her husband and donkey, accepting no money except the occasional present, and not considering herself as being employed. But she got company, an audience for her rambling reminiscences, and an escape from home life with Costa. She repaid us in affection and sweetness of nature. She loved our grandchildren, chattered cheerfully in Greek to our British friends, and on special occasions wrote us artless and oddly spelt verses of good wishes.

Irene, some thirty years younger, had no scruples about offering her services at the going market rate, or higher if she could get it. She worked by the day, alternating between us and Marily's brother Stevie, in the old house over the wall. She lived in the upper village – known locally, though not on maps, as Pahatika – with her bus-driver husband and their son, who was about to do his military service. She walked the kilometre to work each morning. She was a sturdy, good-looking young woman, with black hair and wide green eyes in a pansy-shaped face, and a thorough worker. She was also bossy and touchy and, like Olga, could not resist talking loudly and incessantly to anyone within earshot. When by herself in the house she sang.

Irene was, however, no ordinary servant. Her father had been overseer on the estate known as St John of the Pigeons, overlooking the east coast between Benitses and Moraitika. The family of seven girls grew up to be almost completely self-sufficient, growing or rearing everything they ate, except coffee and sugar, evaporating sea water to produce salt, and manufacturing the bricks with which they built the bread oven. As a result Irene was the complete country woman. She knew in detail which wild vegetables could be cut for salads, which berries and fungus were safe to eat. She was an expert gardener, both of flowers and vegetables, and could use the *tsapa*, or mattock, with the strength of a man, or as delicately as sugar-tongs for transplanting young strawberries. She was, in fact, happier working in our garden than in the house. Her cooking was robust and tasty, usually based on a whole chopped head of garlic, yet she presented all dishes with an innately artistic eye. It was this love of beauty, apparent also in her arrangement of flowers, which outshone all other qualities and defects.

It found an outlet, too, in inter-related feelings for music and religion. Irene's voice was true and pure, but untrained except in the esoteric art of Byzantine liturgical singing. This she knew simply at the level of our village church choir, which never achieved much technical mastery and could sink to painful, but endearing, depths of rustic incompetence, or even total breakdown. (This was largely due to the fact that Gerasimos, the chief psaltis, and Irene's mentor, was now in his eighties and prone to miss both pitch and place.) But she took her role seriously, and practised *kontakia* in our hall and bedrooms.

Irene's religiosity seemed, sometimes, to border on the obsessive. Olga, of a generation for which the pattern of the year was set by the saints' days and major festivals of the Church calendar, and to which the miracles of popular hagiology seemed entirely natural, was no less an unquestioning believer, but wore her religion in an easier and more matter-of-fact way. One morning I offered to give her a lift into town. As we started, Olga made the sign of the Cross, saying, 'As we have begun, so may we finish. My neighbour always says that before she starts to dig – because of snakes, you know.' We drove down the main road, and at the second bend the passenger door flew open. Olga shut it with a bang. 'A good thing', she said, 'that I crossed myself, or I would have fallen out.' Later, she told Marily that in her youth there had been two fierce dogs near that bend in the road, and that she had been nervous about walking past them. To protect herself she would show them the gold cross which hung round her neck, for she knew that they were not real dogs, but evil spirits.

Hussein the donkey had been named after the Jordanian monarch, because, according to his mistress, he did no work, was waited on hand and foot, and lived like a king. He was more than twenty years old, and semi-retired, but still carried burdens when Olga visited any of her three little properties, and gave rides to visiting small children. On being let out of his stable in the morning he liked first to roll on the ground,waving his hooves in the air, like a puppy. Olga kept him in excellent condition – he was almost her only piece of moveable property – and professed, like the priestess of an oracle, to interpret his utterances. These took but one form, a winding-up crescendo of despairing whoops, leading to three or four brays of heart-rending anguish, often accompanied by a triumphant breaking of wind. 'He heard me coming,' Olga would say, or 'He wants some water' or 'He's calling for a bride, but he's past it, of course.'

The other most frequent, if spasmodic, member of the *prosopiko* – the personnel – was Spiro the Father-in-Law. We and he acquired each other a few years earlier, when we were building a retaining wall for the new front garden. The mason and his mate needed an extra labourer, and Marily undertook to provide one. Inquiries in the village led to evasive replies and a strong indication that nobody, however able-bodied, would demean himself to mix cement for anybody else. At last, out of a fog-bank of hints and circumlocutions there floated the name of a character, referred to variously as Pipinos, or as O Petheros (which means the Father-in-Law), whom it might possibly (but don't say I said so) be worth approaching. Marily tracked him down. He turned out to be a retired policeman, of dignified aspect, living in Pahatika. At the end of a tortuous conversation, tactfully disguising the fact that he had been tipped off about our interest, he promised that, for an agreed wage, he would be on the spot at eight o'clock on Tuesday morning, ready to start work. Should he be prevented, he would send a substitute. At eight o'clock on Tuesday morning, mason and mate were there, but neither O Petheros nor a replacement. By good fortune we found a young man who was taking a day off from re-tiling a neighbour's roof, and the work proceeded. That evening Marily found the Father-in-Law at home and reproached him. He was sorry, he had been unavoidably prevented. Reminded that he had undertaken to send someone in his place, he said calmly, 'Well, you found someone, didn't you?' 'No thanks to you,' said my wife. 'Well, anyway,' he said, 'have some mulberries', and produced a bowlful, newly picked from his tree.

Next morning he was the first on the scene, and demanded to know where the others were. Having made the point that he was no wage slave, more a Greek Alfred Doolittle, he worked steadily until the wall was completed. In conversation he let it fall, in the villagers' usual roundabout manner, that he might, if he had time and inclination, help to clear broom and other scrub from our hillside. The arrangement suited us well. It turned out that Spiro was the local gravedigger (his humour was in the true tradition), and he was clearly proud of his strength, which for his seventy years was remarkable. He split logs with an axe so heavy that I could hardly lift it above my shoulder. But he was careful to harbour his powers, and never worked longer than a five-hour day. He more than once expounded his theory that the body is a delicate machine which imposes its own limits, and must be humoured to function aright. (His own engine, it soon became obvious, needed topping-up with regular and frequent injections of alcohol.)

We seemed to be the only people to call Spiro by his baptismal name, and not by either of his nicknames, both of which had ancient and obscure origins. This was in line with a widespread village use of the *paratsoukli*, or nickname. A new hotel at the foot of the hill was called the Bintzan, which was simply the owner's *paratsoukli*, while the Botsi clan were not Botsis at all, their official name, very common in the village, being Kondos (in English, 'Short'). So, a funeral notice, posted up on telegraph poles, would read 'Nikolaos Kondos (Botsi)'. Irene was vulgarly known as Tsoutsaina, which means baby's bottle.

Another prominent *paratsouklian* was our old friend Mantou. One of the island's ubiquitous Spiros, Mantou was a patriarchal figure of old village stock, who owned a large property beside the Perama road, beyond Kopanous. By energy and acumen he had become prosperous, and maintained a vigorous independence from the easy-going village, whose inhabitants have long had a reputation for considering hard work beneath their dignity. His wife Olga was a strong-jawed woman, who still wore the traditional long skirt, white blouse, and kerchief of the countrywoman. Abroad, she carried a smart modern hand-bag, the badge of her opinion – openly expressed and completely accurate – that she was as good as any of the gentry. They and their two married sons, and a troop of grandchildren, inhabited a cluster of houses on the property, alive with dogs, hens and goats.

Mantou had had a close relationship, all his life, with Marily's family, and had known her since they were children. He never failed to call on us, bringing with him a demi-john of home-produced wine as hearty and positive as himself. His appearances in the village were mainly in the capacity of master of ceremonies at religious processions – a role which he also exercised at the litanies of the Saint in town.

Old Olga's rosebud, Costa, was generally known in the village as 'Tsatteras', a nickname which we learned of only at the time of his death, some years later. At the time of which I am writing, he was entering on his last slow decline. He no longer drank, but was fit for little but to drag himself on sunny days to the street, where he used to sit on a low wall, wearing a woollen cap and smoking cigarettes. Eventually he had a fall and was taken to hospital with a broken thigh. There he developed gangrene in his leg, and it was amputated. He never left his bed, lingering for several weeks until he died. Olga stayed at his bedside day and night, occasionally relieved for a few hours by one of their daughters. It is doubtful if he realised that his leg had gone, but its loss was a cause of serious anxiety to his wife that he might not be admitted to Paradise with only one.

Tsatteras's body was brought to the village, and lay in his open coffin in a little church on the main street, attended by all his large family in deep black from head to foot. The whole community visited to pay their respects. Death had restored peace and dignity to the old man's ravaged face. Next day, the cemetery church was packed. At the climax of the service, when the priest advanced with incense to say the last prayers over the body, the women of the family broke into shrill lamentations, and one collapsed heavily to the floor. Later accounts of the ceremony were enlivened with the embellishment that they had all fainted simultaneously. It was agreed that he got a send-off worthy of one who had been a warrior in his time and had undoubtedly fathered several extra children in the district.

We could always call for help in emergency from Spiro and Nina Kamareli (yet another *paratsoukli*), who lived in an ancestral house opposite our gate. Spiro was, I think, the only man in the village who made a living from agriculture. He owned, and worked single-handed, a small farm about a mile away, which he walked to and from every day. As well as growing vegetables and fruit, he kept goats and hens and fed his family from the surplus. Nina was a rough tough illiterate girl from Kynopiastes, the village of the Dogcatchers, across the valley. On party nights she would make a whirlwind assault on our washing-up, having announced her arrival to the company by whistling at the front door. She was immensely strong and looked capable of making a meal of her small husband, whom she always referred to as her *kyrios* – as one might say, her lord and master.

We did our best to maintain easy relations, not only with the Kamarelis, but with all our near neighbours along the lane. At the top there lived Vasilo, a rumbustious spinster with a facial resemblance to Tenniel's Duchess and a taste for red wine and very short skirts – a late reaction, perhaps, to years of having had to care for an invalid father. Opposite her, for part of the year, was Kyria Anna, a widow of Asia Minor origin. She had become old and heavy, but was still capable of enlivening a party by wearing a mask and performing a rapidly quivering belly-dance.

Below Kyria Anna lived an elderly couple, Spiro and Koula, who also kept a donkey, though not on our land, and a fat, obsequious bitch of no known breed, called Penelope. She was a gifted scrounger, with an unrivalled nose for cooked meat. When we came back from eating out, she would follow the car to our door in the expectation that we would have brought her scraps.

Next door, and older still, was Vasili, with his nice wife Zaira. He was a serious and dignified man. He had been a carpenter, but his status derived mainly from his former position for many years as director and conductor of the village wind band. He took great pride in its performance and appearance, especially when it took its accustomed place in the processions of St Spyridon in town. By dedication and discipline Vasili had made it an honour for a village boy to be accepted as a trumpet or horn player, or a shrill clarinettist, and equally a disgrace to be dismissed for bad behaviour. Now he was a village elder, of the best sort.

Lastly, where the lane reached the main road, lay Leonidas's and Leni's house. They had had a connection with the Bulgaris all their lives. Leni was Mantou's sister, a simple, gentle, unlettered soul – later to lose her sight and her spirit. Leonidas harvested our olives for us, taking, of course, the major part of the crop, and keeping an eye on Kapoutsi during the winter. We returned with gratitude to our small community.

4

Sophia

Just after Easter we had a visitation from our other world, in the person of Sophia. Sophia was as true blue a Corfiot villager as either Olga or Irene, but she had become part of our life many years earlier and in a very different context. Her native village was Chlomos, high on the mountain which springs steeply from the coast, beyond the river valley of Mesonghi. It was, and is, a proud and private place. The road zig-zags interminably up the stony hillside and leads only to the village. Once there, it is just possible to drive a little way to the miniature *plateia*. Beyond that one goes on foot along lanes which twist between the tight-packed houses. Since the Middle Ages the Chlomians have looked out over the sea from their pirate-proof stronghold, and express disdain for the parvenus of the valley bottom.

Sophia and her sisters, daughters of the village butcher, had grown up in this enclosed society, moulded by the lore and custom of generations, word-perfect in the prayers and hymns of their church, attending the demotic primary school, and from the age of twelve joining the older women to work in the *kambo* – the wide plain at the mountain foot, covered by olivegroves, vineyards, pasture land and fields of corn and vegetables. Each morning early, all the able-bodied women and girls would set off down the hill, to return each evening, either trudging barefoot or riding those horses and donkeys not required to carry firewood, fodder or farm produce.

Chlomos, like most Corfiot villages of any size, had a relic of the feudal past, an *archontiko spiti* – what would be known in Scotland as the 'big house' – belonging to a family which had once exercised rights of superiority over the ordinary folk of the district. The lady of this manor was Sophia's godmother, who became increasingly worried about her well-being after she had grown up. Her mother had died and her father re-married, and she did not get on with her stepmother. Her sisters had in turn married and left the family home. Sophia herself was in love with a boy who wanted to marry her, but her father, the archetypal village patriarch, forebade the match. Sophia showed signs of becoming desperate.

About the same time, we had created the house on the shore at Mesonghi where we were to spend so many summer holidays. Sophia's godmother was an old friend of Ina and the two of them came up with the idea that we might employ her and take her to Scotland, to escape completely from her home environment. The suggestion came temptingly. We had just parted company from Anna, a hardworking and intelligent Corinthian girl who had worked for us in Edinburgh for a year. She had a passionate nature which she let loose upon the cellarman of a local wine merchant. The affair began well, but to Anna's uncomprehending dismay, when she took to biting his thighs he got cold feet and threw her over. Unfortunately, she had less endearing habits, and when we discovered that she was building a trousseau from our household linen and silver she had to go. We were wary of repeating the experiment, but we agreed to meet Sophia. She came down to Mesonghi with her little horse, called Boy, and gave the children rides along the beach, and won us all with her humour and good nature.

So in the autumn Sophia had been taken to Athens and put on a train (the first she had ever seen) for the three-day journey across Europe. In London she was met and put on another train, and arrived in Edinburgh, in her village garb, speaking no word of any language but Greek, and dauntless for a new life.

That life she shared with Marily and me, our three children and my old mother, giving always more than she took, for nine years. She quickly learned to speak serviceable English, saved her money, and bought a flat large enough for her to let rooms – mostly to Greeks studying in the city, many of whom came to regard her almost as a mother. Her cooking, especially of Greek dishes, became renowned and was much in demand. Although she never married she became a popular character with all our friends, and in her own district, as well as being a faithful supporter of the local Orthodox church, whose worship remained for her a beloved necessity.

Identification with all that Chlomos had comprised inevitably weakened with the years. To begin with the sisters corresponded regularly, exchanging their news – a family trick – in rhyming couplets. The letters grew scarcer; Sophia became townified in dress and hair style, and picked up Scottish ways. The point of no return, perhaps, was the day when she was naturalised as a British citizen, putting the seal on a foreigner's metamorphosis into an accepted and respected member of the Edinburgh community. She welcomed and returned the love and appreciation which she found there, but there was a certain sadness in it, too. When her father died, Sophia inherited the family house in the village. She went back to take it over, with a hope that she might make her home in it, but it was too late. She had outgrown the old customs and the easy companionship which had once fitted her like a garment. There seemed to be no place for her as an unmarried, westernised woman on the verge of middle age. She modernised the house for letting to the foreign holidaymakers, and returned to her adopted country.

It was during one of Sophia's annual visits to Chlomos that, almost thirty years after we first met her, she came to lunch with us at Kapoutsi, accompanied by her elderly Scottish friend, Christine. Irene had cooked for us spicy *keftedhes* and created two artistic salads, a green one of lettuce leaves arranged in the form of a huge flower, and cold brown beans adorned with small white rings of onion. At the start of the meal Sophia asked us all to stand and sing the 'Christos Anesti' – 'Christ is risen from the dead'. Irene made sure that we folded our hands properly in front of us, and then led the singing in her strong, church-choir voice, looking straight ahead with her wide green eyes. We began by cracking (à la mode of conkers) and eating the red-dyed hard-boiled eggs of Eastertide. After lunch Irene insisted that the shells must be scattered in the garden, not mixed with the rest of the rubbish, because they had been sanctified as part of the Feast, and symbolised the Resurrection.

We drove Sophia and Christine to Chlomos. It poured on the way, and was still dripping gently at the village. We walked with them to the house and left them in a green shade of walnut and mulberry, with a watery southward view past Petriti and the salt-pans of Alikes, to the gulf.

5

The Village

The Corfu building boom was showing no sign of decline. On many of the coastal hillsides, housing estates had taken over the olive groves which had been their charm. When we looked out from our terrace, we began to fear that we would soon be nothing but a garden suburb of the town. Every landowner, however humble, was either building or about to build, for letting, or investment, or, it sometimes seemed, just to keep up with the Ioannous.

Our own villagers were not immune from the fever, but they built mostly on their outlying properties near the sea. The village itself remained, in essence, as we had always known it. Some of the picturesque, poky old houses were being pulled down and replaced by new ones with light, space and modern sanitation, but the overall character was unchanged.

At the entrance to the village, the road from town forked. A signpost invited the traveller either to turn right for Platanos, or to take the left-hand road to the casino. (These instructions were peculiarly confusing to strangers, most of whom were there by accident, having earlier missed their way to the south and unaware either that that there was a casino in the vicinity or that Platanos means plane tree.) The road to the left continued uphill and was the main thorough-fare, leading to the Bella Vista and then steeply down to the coast. To the right, one descended to the older, more private part of the village.

After passing the community office and rural surgery, this road slanted down the side of a steep ravine and then turned abruptly left. The corner was overlooked by a house with a *bodzo* – a first-floor covered porch reached by an outside stair – on which sat Ourano, the widow Urania, with her crochet work, benignly monitoring all our goings out and comings in. At the same corner, stout Costa, the butcher with the Stalinite moustache, ran a small *kafeneion*, patronised by Spiro the Father-in-Law and the church sacristan, a placid man with a pipe and spectacles called Kimon. From there a pedestrian alley led down to the church, between some of the oldest and most dilapidated houses.

The Church of the Odhiyitria was perched on a terraced platform, below which the hill plunged steeply again to the valley bottom. It used to possess a tiny graveyard, with a clear view to the hilltop and cypress-ringed chapel of Ayia Kyriaki. Marily and I had had a fancy to be laid to rest there together, but a couple of years earlier Papa Thanassi, in the course of his whirlwind incumbency, dug up all the bodies, re-buried them in a new vulgar cemetery, and covered the little God's Acre with cement, for use on social occasions.

Along from Costa's corner, a stack of olive-wood logs betrayed the existence of a *fourno*, or oven – the bakery over which Ektoras had presided for many years. He and his pretty wife Eleni – a modern Hector and Helen – lived above the shop. Swallows had built nests under an intervening ledge, and in spring decorated the shop-front with a frieze of gaping beaks. Except on Sundays, Hector baked the village's daily bread, and nothing but bread, rising at four to prepare his loaves and heat the big wood-fired oven. By ten a comforting yeasty smell told that the first loaves were about to emerge, first the white and then the brown, circular *leftes*, long rectangular *formes* and the twisted *striftes* preferred by most of his customers. His bread had won Hector a reputation all over the island, and his traditional methods even attracted foreign journalistic attention. His picture, dapper in baker's apron and flat white cap, together with Eleni's smiling face framed in her kerchief, had featured in several magazines.

Opposite the *fourno*, old Dimo ran a humble café-cum-shop with a faded fresco above the door of flowers and trees, painted by the artist who decorated the Empress Elisabeth's little palace a hundred years before. Dimo never had much to sell, but he had an excellent line in salted hake, a staple of the village diet. His café was patronised by Pater Spiro Perdikas – Father Partridge, but Papa Pipi to old friends – now retired after many years as parish priest, and a childhood friend of Marily. He still walked up to the village of a morning for a coffee at Dimo's and a chat with old parishioners. Always wearing his black *raso* and *kamilafki*, the priest's cassock and chimney-pot hat, he could be seen on a stone bench opposite the café with three or four kerchiefed women, like a crow among pigeons. (Our current priest, the King Log to Papa Thanasi's King Stork, was another Papa Spiro, who had returned to his native island after many years in charge of the Greek Orthodox congregation in Cardiff. Both he and his wife had become too westernised for the villagers' conservative taste. He was censured as '*modernos*' for wearing swimming trunks in the sea, and shorts for gardening. Church people, whether British or Greek, are hard to please.)

That was the end of the main village. The road then meandered along the hillside, crossed a bridge over another small ravine, and climbed again to the Platanos of the sign-post, a plane tree of immense girth, below which a spring of clean sweet water had always flowed out of the hill. As late as the 1950s this was, apart from wells, the village's only water supply, and may have determined its original siting. About 1890 the Empress Elisabeth, whose palace was nearby, took an interest in the welfare of the village, and improved the spring by installing pipes and troughs for washing clothes. She surmounted her work with a pious verse, in marble, from the Orthodox hymnary and an inscription commemorating her own name. A flight of steps climbed from the road to a second, equally enormous plane. Years ago a crazed old woman lived in its hollow base, which resembled a small round cell complete with crude doorway and window. Despite their age the two trees showed no sign of failing, and fragrantly shaded the spring from the summer heat.

Olga was fond of recalling the evenings of her youth, when the women and girls gathered at the spring to draw water and exchange news. They met all their friends, and chattered and laughed while waiting their turn to fill their jugs and pots. Then they would help each other to balance the receptacles on their heads (with a quoit of twisted cloth for protection), and wend homewards in twos and threes, holding themselves very erect and swaying only at the hips, so as not to spill a drop. Sometimes, Olga said, if she met a friend who was on her way to the *platano* she would pour away her water and go back for more, just for a gossip. All that was finished now. The spring had been partly diverted into a public mains supply, but there were still three taps to which people came from all over to draw the cold sweet water – the right accompaniment to a warm crust of Hector's bread.

At its top end, the steep glen of the valley opened into a green basin of orange trees. Where the road skirted round these, the scent of the blossom could be almost too sweet to bear. A side road led to the cemetery and on to a quarry from which builders' lorries constantly brought gravel through the village, and then one was in Pahatika. Although the small settlement had no official independent existence, that was not the view of its inhabitants. Nor did it feel like a mere appendage of the village, at which it stared boldly across a leafy gulf. It did not possess a shop or *kafeneion*, but it had its own working parish church, its Sunday services alternating with those in the Odhiyitria. There was also an olive-pressing plant serving the whole village. This was owned and run by Alexandros, neighbour of his brother Taki (short for Socrataki, the diminutive of Socrates), the village *proedros*, or president. The latter was a man with a considerable talent for inertia, except where his own interests were involved. It was something of a feat, as a New Democracy conservative, to be elected president of our resolutely PASOK community.

Spiro the Father-in-Law lived by the entrance to Pahatika. Irene's house was at the far end, close to a tiny church dedicated to an obscure St Marcian. Here she kept an abundant garden and a harem of hens towering over, but ruled by, a bantam cock. Beyond, the hamlet ended and the road became a rude track, through woods and heather banks, to the valley bottom. At this point the optimistic tourist would realise that he was in a cul-de-sac and go back to try his luck on the road to the left.

This was the public face of the village. It was also its spine, from which a network of alleys and stairways threaded the jumble of houses, yards and small gardens on either side – down to the lower road and up to the pinnacle and church of the Taxiarchs, the Archangels in command of the heavenly armies.

A blind S-bend brought one first to the Syllogo, an assembly hall of classical design used for formal meetings and receptions, but doubling as the headquarters and practice room of the band. On the other side of the road a legend, and a logo of a rising sun, crudely depicted in green, proclaimed the local office of the left-wing political party, PASOK. (The rival establishment of the New Democracy, a couple of hundred yards up the road, favoured blue for its notices, thus dividing the village, on Byzantine lines, between the Blue and Green factions.)

The guardian of this socialist shrine was Spiro the Croupier, who lived with his family next door. A young man of surly good looks, he was so firm in his beliefs that he displayed on the dashboard of his car a PASOK membership card, complete with photograph of the beloved leader, Andreas Papandreou. When not assisting the collapse of capitalism by raking in the stakes of the idle rich, Spiro spent most of his spare time in building a substantial house, not far from ours. This he did practically with his own hands, transporting the materials on the back of a motor-cycle or on his mother's donkey along a narrow footpath to the site. The operation was illegal. No building permit could have been issued for a house without vehicular access to a public road. But PASOK having been in power when he started, and local government politics being what they were, this was not, perhaps, an impediment. In any case, so many unauthorised houses had been built that the town hall had long since abandoned any pretence of enforcing the regulations. (Sophia's younger sister, it is true, did serve a sentence of a month's imprisonment for erecting a small seaside grill, The Almond Tree, without permission. She thought this a worthwhile alternative to demolition, and reported that conditions in a women's jail were tolerable.)

The street then curved without a footway, past a terrace of houses which included Spiro Kondos's *kafeneion*, and a general store kept by the Widow Spinoula. The café must have been one of the least attractive in Greece. It provided nowhere to sit outside, unless one counted the stone ledge against the outer wall on which perched those waiting for the bus to town. The interior was dingy and poorly lit by two small windows, and devoid of decoration except one outsize poster of a pouting page-three girl with phenomenal breasts. Spiro was a dour little man, with a head too big for his body. As accompaniment to the drink she kept a sack of unshelled peanuts, which he doled out by the handful. His clients, as morose as he was, played endless games of cards, and were reckoned to be solid PASOK supporters. None of them was ever seen at church.

We had at one time become very familiar with the inside of the café. For several years after occupying Kapoutsi we had difficulty in obtaining a telephone. Neither charm nor medical certificates made any impression on the official dealing with such applications. Casually dressed and bearded like Fidel Castro, he soon revealed himself to be a PASOK commissar with the duty of denying a telephone to anyone not an active combatant in the Workers' Struggle. We had therefore no choice but to use the village public phone, located in Spiro's café. To get an outside line often took up to half an hour, which one passed in a smelly open cupboard, in view and hearing of the card-players.

Amalia, the widow woman next door, had inherited the shop from her husband. It occupied her days but did not seem to bring her much cheer. She could read neither letters nor figures and depended on her neighbours' help and customers' honesty. She stayed in business by selling only non-perishable goods – mainly sweets, cigarettes, black garbage disposal bags, soft drinks and ouzo and by having no overheads. The shop was the postman's delivery point for all village mail, and sported a yellow post-box. Our commercial district ended a few yards further on at a rival, rather more convincing shop, run by an elderly ex-pedlar and his wife.

The street then became open and tree-lined as far as the crossroads at the obelisk of the Heroes, recording the names – so many Kondos, Pahis and Spinoulas – of those who died for the fatherland in the Balkan wars. The area comprised, as well, the primary school (under the charge of old Vasili's son-in-law) and a large paved *plateia*, used on two main occasions in the year: for communal merrymaking on the night of the village Paniyiri in August; and for the reading of the Resurrection Gospel at midnight on Easter Eve; when the new light is borne in procession from the church with band and choir, and there are fireworks and kissing all round.

We had recently acquired, at the crossroads, our first restaurant, a grill room specialising in chops, kebabs, chips and salad, and little else. This had been opened, not by any of the villagers, for whom such a display of mercantile initiative would have been undignified, but by Lefteri, a lean and enterprising incomer from Epirus across the water. Smelling a potential profit from the passing tourist trade, he advertised the premises in both English and German, and incidentally gave the locals, at last, an agreeable eating place on summer evenings.

Thence the main road led out of the village towards the coast. An attractive road to the left wandered down the ridge, past Kopanous and Mantou's property and Cecil and Fanny Lewis's house, to the roaring holiday delights of Perama. To the right a rough track pointed the way to the hilltop of Ayia Kyriaki, where the unhappy empress used to seek consolation in prayer.

6

Leaves from a Kapoutsi Journal

Wednesday, 3 May A heavy, still Corfiot day, threatening rain, but none till evening. Unpacked, got the house into shape and began on the garden. The trees, shrubs and flowers are all in good health – roses in full bloom, the red bougain-vilias magnificent – but half swamped by clover and other weeds. The drive is a mess. But all lovely. Broom in yellow flower down the hillside, and lots of scabious and purple vetch. Because of the very warm winter and spring, iris and orchids almost over, except for the pink pyramidal. We have some apricots, for the first time, on the young trees and some cherries, and – at last – a few of the old almond trees have nuts again. Not a bad olive crop. The fruit is still mostly on the trees.

Our swallows are back and in and out of the nest in the porch, which looks dilapidated. Vasilo came by, with two cats, and George and Elena came to greet us and had tea. Then M. and I went into town to see her father, who is well and on the spot. Supped at Chrysi's taverna. A cold night.

Friday, 5 May At dawn the last owls and the first tits were singing together. Time 6.15 (we are about 4 degrees, or 15 minutes in time, behind Athens). The owls were two scops, not well synchronised, and a tone different in pitch – the higher one having the quicker beat.

The Kamareli family, at the gate, in great disarray because 'my master', as Nina calls her Spiro, is in hospital with terrible stomach pains and everyone, including Spirouli himself, thinks he is dying. They are, like all the villagers, dedicated hypochondriacs, but he is a nice little man, and a good farmer, and Nina though rough and grasping is a helpful neighbour, so we are being supportive. Sunset, fiery, at 8.35.

Sunday, 7 May (of St Thomas) Went to church. A large choir – four men, two women and a small girl – who made, for our village, a harmonious noise. Then joined the Litaneia (the procession through the village). It used to go well beyond, to the Rizikari church, but now only as far as the Bella Vista. Old Vasili's grandson, Billy, in his first year in the band, playing kettle-drum, and Gerasimos's boy on a horn of sorts. We found George and Elena near the top and came home in their car. Poor weather, but good to see the familiar, light-eyed village faces.

Then drove to Kalami, for lunch with Greg and Aleka Panas. Their house is practically on the beach, next to the White House, of Durrell fame. A real old-Corfiot mob: Greg's older brother John and his Roxani, Winnie Skoura and Yuri, Manoli and Stefi Zolota, Sotiri and Nena Boufidis, Andrea and Aspasia Botti, Aleko and Kiki Chimarrio (their daughter has finished at Cambridge and has started practising law in Piraeus), George and Elena, and us. I the only *xenos*. It had been dull and rainy on the way, but the weather moved across to Epirus, and suddenly the Albanian coast was very near and clear. With binoculars one could make out what looked like a pleasant red-roofed village. Perhaps they are human after all.

After lunch we walked by a narrow path to the next bay, a charming horseshoe of light shingle, fringed with yellow horned poppies and agaves. Stratified cliffs, with big rock shelves, at the far end. Nobody else there except a girl disconsolately taking photographs, while her mate took a siesta. From the appearance of his forearms, tattooed in woad with daggers and dragons, I took him to be a Briton.

Back home, it had become brilliant *maîstro* weather, with the whole Albanian range clearly visible. New snow on the high tops. We lit the fire, as well as the Jøtul stove, and needed both. George and Elena, and M's cousin Niki, came for a snack supper, and we were very easy.

Tuesday, 9 May Called on the Kamarelis, to find Spiro back home, looking the picture of health. Going to the village, we complimented old Vasili on his oranges; on our way back, he presented us with a big bagful, plus a few lemons. He says that the almond crop is good everywhere, for no clear reason, after a number of lean years. Harvesting the almonds used to be a serious annual event here, and also up at Vasiliko – where M.'s grandmother and Aunt Silvia went every August and stayed for a week. . . After lunch we went 'down the mountain', as Olga says, to the hillside property above Benitses where she has olive trees. She also looks after the little house and garden where Peter and Steve stayed when not running the American school in London (their local nickname was the *nerokokori*, or waterfowl). We found her filling basins with shining black olives. Hussein was nibbling at the grass but accepted the bread we had brought for him. The gulf was a sheet of very pale blue and pinky yellow, from the Fortress to the salt pans. Olga loves the place and draws unusual serenity from the countryside. We collected ferns and myrtles for the garden, and five sacks of oak leaf mould.

A cold evening. We lit fires and supped off spinach pie and Irene's wine – young and strong and free from harmful additives, like its maker. Nina dropped in bearing freshly boiled goat's milk and a new goat cheese, and yelled at us about her family woes. Outside, the fireflies were zipping about to keep warm. Could hear a nightingale far down in the valley.

Cecil and Fanny Lewis are back from London.

Thursday, 11 May The swallows are still fussing around, in and out of the porch all day, repairing their ramparts. This morning one of them flew into the house and kept on bashing into the picture window, in spite of my efforts to divert it. In the end, had to pick it up, half knocked out, and put it out. Marvellous metallic blue.

p.m. We went with George and Elena, and Petro their eldest, to Ay. Yianni for the FIRST SWIM, though M. funked it. Beastly cold, but delicious in the sun after. Counter-attacked a nasty invasion of couch grass.

Friday, 12 May A somewhat depressing lunch at the Bulgaris. The Count* was very low. The meal was scarcely over before the family drifted to the living room to watch an imbecilic American soap opera, to which the whole population is addicted.

The Lewises called at drinks time and we kept them for a left-over supper. He has had his book launched, and appeared on TV with Wogan, and on radio with Ned Sherrin, and is as pleased as Punch. For ninety-two he is quite amazing. While in England he visited his eighty-eight-year-old stepmother, with whom he says he gets on well. She was his father's third wife, as Fanny is his. A good evening.

Saturday, 13 May Something has happened to our swallows. Since last night there has been no amorous chatter from the porch, and only one bird around, sitting gloomily above the door or on the telephone wire. I suspect that the one I rescued may have suffered brain damage. An ill-starred couple. Last year the whole nest fell down, brood and all, and now this.

Sunday, 14 May Hot, heavy and windy. M. painted, I gardened. Then to church for Spiro and Koula Bogdanou's grandson's christening. About fifty there, mostly women. The child got the full Orthodox treatment of three complete immersions, anointings, etc., and everything was incessantly

*Count Spiridon Bulgaris, my father-in-law.

photographed and videoed. Distasteful, but now the rage at weddings and so on. The babe objected loudly throughout. His mother, who is English, thought it all awful, and her mother also 'disapproved'. What, one wonders, did they expect?

M. and I walked to Kopanous, making a circuit to the top of the village past some pleasant old houses and properties, up a steep bank to Koukoutsi, where M. used to play as a child, and then down through olives to the orchid field beside the Kopanous road. Many varieties in flower. Back home, found the Kamarelis with sacks full of olives. The harvest, a good one, if late, is in full swing everywhere. It is one of the climaxes of the year, of age-old significance.

Watered, and sowed zinnias and flower-of-the-veldt. Finally up to Lefteri's *psistaria* for pork *souvlakia*. The only other customers were a friendly German couple, who ordered a bottle of red wine, nothing else. Lefteri's son thoughtfully brought the Kouros, the most expensive on his list, which they polished off and left. We were attended by two dogs, one elderly, with an air of faded nobility, like a Corfiot gentleman of the old school. The other was robust and vigorous, with a heavy but interesting head, and was named Ozal, after the Turkish P.M.

A good village day. We have seen and talked to a lot of people and their dogs. Tonight another swallow has appeared, and the double bed seems to be occupied.

Monday, 15 May Expelled a four-inch millipede from the bathroom, like a self-propelled shoe lace, one of evolution's little jokes.

Went for a haircut to the barber Cecil and I share, Yanko Hytiri at Kouramades. (Cecil has never attempted to master Greek, and calls the village Dolmades, anglice stuffed cabbage leaves.) Shop as spick as ever, with two vases of red roses. Kyr Yanko told me how his career began. When he was about twenty he came across a village woman weeping

because her two little boys had been sent home from school
for having their hair too long, and she had no money to send
them to town. He went home, got a pair of scissors and a
comb, dragged the children out of their kitchen, set them on
a bench outside, and cut their hair. An old man passing asked
to have his hair cut, and while this was being done another
man offered to take Yanko to Corfu town – if he was inter-
ested – and introduce him to a barber to learn the trade. He
agreed and, forty-five years later, is still shaving and cutting
hair in his native village. 'I know everyone,' he said, 'their
joys and their sorrows. What a pity Kyrios Lewis can't speak
any Greek. I could tell him all about my career, and he could
write it down.'

A perfect swim at A.Y. in the afternoon. Calm, clear
water, a network of gold shifting across ribbed sand, a gentle
breeze, no tourist caiques, only three or four other couples.

After dark, fireflies all over the garden, and a high white
gibbous moon. The last day of my sixty-ninth year, a happy
one for us both.

Tuesday, 16 May A funny frog birthday card from M. Irene
appeared with a spray of red roses and carmine carnations,
in silver foil. 'For thee, from me,' she said, kissing me
generously on both cheeks. She also brought *skordalia* garlic
sauce, the idea being, presumably, that I should smell as
lovely as I look.

We drove to Foundana, to see if Denis and Pauline Rickett
had arrived from England – they had, a fortnight ago, but
have no phone. He is very lame from his bad knee, but
managed to drive his big car all the way. Came back by the
Val di Ropa. Picked a large bunch of blood red wayside
poppies and yellow crown daisies.

Cecil and Fanny came and drank my health in brandy. He
gave me a signed copy of *The Gospel according to Judas*. Picked
tiny Corfu strawberries, and some artichokes, from Stevie's
garden. A bundle of boring mail, plus a nice letter from Eola.

Wednesday, 17 May Delayed birthday lunch. Niki, her brother George Ralli (the ex-P.M.) and Lena, Winnie and Yuri (pleased to be included), and M.'s brother Sergio – his Maria is in Paris. He undertook to have the Kopanous pool cleaned and filled by the summer holidays.

Jack and Ann came on the late plane from Athens. Brought a good drawing of a hilltop Byzantine church.

Thursday, 18 May Leonidas thinned the Isabella vines on the lower pergola. He says the young grapes need more air.

We took Jack and Ann to Hector's *fourno* and introduced them. Bought bread and went on to Pahatika to watch the olive pressing at Alexandros's *litrouvio*. We were given thick slices of fresh bread, with newly pressed oil to dip them in. Washed down with Aleko's own wine, the ace of elevenses.

Thence to Kombitsi, where M. had a dressmaker's fitting, and we walked down the ancient paved way to the Vaska, the elegant Venetian spring below the old house. Then on to Liapades. Ate *sofrito* at the Nychterida taverna ('the Bat'), pleasant and friendly as always. Village women rode past on donkeys, all wearing a distinctive kind of light blue sun-bonnet. The tables had new plastic cloths, specially designed for the tourist trade, with blue pictures of lambs on spits, and mounds of fruit, and the legend 'Kali Orexi: Bon Apetit. Goog Appettite.'

It was cool all day, and we lit a fire in the evening. Spiro the Father-in-Law called, bringing fresh eggs and a bag of *nespoles* (loquats) from his tree. 'Picked one by one', he said. How else? He accepted an ouzo, stipulating that it be well chilled, and sat with us, looking splendid with his noble head, and dispensing ironic comments on village life in general, and his daughter's marital problems in particular. Nothing but trouble once you get involved with lawyers, in his opinion. We were sorry to learn that the owner of the BP filling station at Vryoni died a couple of days ago, was put in the fridge, and buried today. Not clear if Spiro dug the grave. He refused a second drink, saying he had to go to the Kafeneion – not little Spiro's, which is too political for his taste, but to 'the Thin One' – to wit, our fat butcher. So away he went, stately on his little motor-scooter.

Sunday, 21 May SS Constantine and Helen. Also Ionian Enosis Day, commemorating the return of the Seven Islands to Greece in 1864. (For three nights, locals are allowed to play at the casino.)

We gave a lunch party in J. and A.'s honour. Ann did the house flowers, beautifully. With Olga and Irene both helping, the kitchen was a babble of Greek chat all morning, except for an interlude of old romantic Corfu songs. Irene has an unusual but very Greek way of singing, without a trace of tremolo. Olga's voice, once very sweet, has become cracked – 'I need winding up,' she said. Lewises and Ricketts, Anthony and Joan Acton, Aleco and Pitsa Dendrino (average age of husbands, eighty-five) Lily Condi, Elizabeth Glenconner and Petro Manessi. Bright sun, but cool and windy on the terrace.

Jack and Ann's last day. They have been impeccable visitors.

Thursday, 25 May To lunch with Elizabeth at Liapades. Dropped off a wedding present for Mantou's granddaughter Olga, on the way. Left the car at The Cricketers at Yefira, and Niko the boatman ferried us to Elizabeth's bay in the Falaina (Whale). Found her on the beach with Denis and Pauline and their daughter and her husband. Invigorating British-type swim, in a cool wind and fitful sunshine. Then lunch on the terrace overlooking the bay. The house, designed by John Collas, is graceful, simple, light and airy, and the garden, in a little valley running back from the beach, a surprise secret world of glades and grey plants and masses of Madonna lilies.

In the evening M. painted a picture. Tomorrow we go to Dodona.

7

Dodona

The day trip to Dodona* was really a piece of un-finished business. A couple of years earlier we had explored Macedonia, in company with our friend Lily Condi. We had intended to end the journey with a detour to Dodona, but on the road down from Metsovo to Ioannina the weather broke in an autumn downpour, and we gave up the idea. Now Lily offered to drive us there and back.

Such an offer was not to be refused lightly. Not only was Lily an old Corfiot friend and agreeable companion; not only was she a good driver; she was also an expert professional guide, speaking perfect English, who had for many years con-ducted coach tours to most of the archaic sites in Greece. We had excellent memories of the Macedonian expedition, which had included some out-of-the-way extras. Lily was anxious to view some recent excavations and especially, if possible, the royal tombs at Vergina brought to light and restored by Professor Andronikos. There we found, as Lily had hoped, that the professor was on site and about to show the tomb of Philip II of Macedon (not open to the public) to a party of Australian archaeologists. We introduced ourselves, and Lily asked if we might tag along. The impresario grumbled, but was, we thought, pleased at the chance to show off to two of his fellow-countrywomen. Thus we gained a private view of the extraordinary burial chamber, and also heard its discoverer tell a well-rehearsed tale of how he had identified both its

---

*The Latin form of the name. In Greek it is Dodone, pronounced Dhodhoni. Dodona is so commonly used, even by scholars, outside Greece that it seems pedantic to insist on the correct form.

location and its occupant. The clinching clue lay in the bones from a golden casket engraved with the sixteen-rayed star of the Macedonian monarchy. One leg was an inch shorter than the other, while the bone above one eye had been fractured at one time. This accorded with contemporary accounts of the king, who walked with a limp and had once been wounded in the eye by an arrow. (The reconstructed skeleton lies, with the tomb treasures, in the Thessaloniki museum.)

We went as far east as the site of Amphipolis, the fifth-century Athenian colony which stood on a ridge, protected on three sides by a slow loop of the River Strymon. There is little left of the city, on the dry windy hilltop, except a corner of the acropolis wall. But in a valley, not far outside the line of the town wall, Lily showed us the foundation piles of an ancient bridge over a former course of the river. Almost certainly this was the very bridge taken in a surprise night attack by the Spartan general Brasidas, its capture enabling him then to take the city as well, as Thucydides tells.

We left Macedonia by way of ancient Dion, on the approach to Mount Olympus, now subject to flooding. A row of melancholy marble ladies stood at the edge of a reed-fringed pool, up to their knees in water. From there we climbed to a high village where Lily was friendly with the owner of the wineshop, and drank his home-made *tsipouro*, the hot-tempered Greek cousin of *marc* and *grappa*, and left Olympus with a two-litre bottle of triple-distilled nectar.

To go to Dodona, we left Kapoutsi at seven and met Lily at the quay for the 7.30 ferry to Igoumenitsa. The drive on the mainland, skirting Ioannina, took us about two hours and a half, through the lush fields and woods of the Kalamas valley, and wide mountain pastures with many flocks of sheep and startlingly tall spikes of yellow verbascum. By noon we were hungry. We went first to the village of Dodona and found a café/general store/post office with two old men sitting in the courtyard beneath a pergola of ten enormous vines. There was no sign of any more inhabitants, other than the friendly woman who supplied us with ouzo and a luncheon-sized *meze* of bread, olives, local cheese in oil, tomatoes, cucumber and hard-boiled eggs. Eaten in tranquillity against a background of red rose bushes, this seemed to us an idyllic appetiser to the unemphatic charm of Dodona's classical site. The grey granite theatre stood solitary in a field of knee-high grass and white and yellow wild flowers. The oak tree of antiquity, the messages of whose rustling leaves was the oldest oracle in all Hellas, is long since gone, but a young oak stands in its place. Nightingales were singing in the wood behind the ruins of an early Christian basilica, and far down the valley a cuckoo called.

We drove to the Ambraciot Gulf down the valley of the Louros. Near the gush of the spring of Louros we found a grassy spot beside a clear stream, haunted by insects somewhere between dragonflies and butterflies, with iridescent blue bodies and dark blue wings. Here we ate a superior picnic with white wine, and saw no human life except a respectable elderly man in a dark suit and shoes who led a small flock of sheep across the stream by a ford. Thence we drove to the Ionian coast and turned northward for home. At Margariti there is an old Turkish fort – once perhaps a warning to the troublesome Greeks of Parga – and a minaret, and we saw three or four families of white storks in huge unkempt nests on various vantage points, including a church belfry. And so to Igoumenitsa and the 5.30 ferry, tired but satisfied.

8

More Leaves from a Kapoutsi Journal

Saturday, 27 May Swam at Ay. Yanni in the morning. At
6.30 to Kopanous for Mantou's Olga's wedding to her
Thomas from Kalafationes. (The engagement party was at
her grandfather's house last autumn, and the baby is due
in September.) The service was in the Sordinas/Palatianos
family chapel, now owned by M.'s brother, Sergios.

A good jolly village affair. The bride was led up the road
from her parents' house with music by a three-piece band –
violin, accordion and guitar. Our Papa Spiro conducted the
service, assisted by the merry young priest from Kalafationes,
who had led the dancing at the engagement party. He fairly
rattles through the prayers and sings with vigour, in contrast to our gentle incumbent. Chapel very crowded. The
usual Orthodox mixture of good-humoured informality and
Byzantine solemnity. The congregational chatter got so loud
that the priests asked people to go outside for conversation,
these being Holy Mysteries. The little bridesmaid's mother
is a nice English girl who married a village boy, and had
Olga as her bridesmaid. She says that Mantou is the best and
kindest man she has ever known.

Olga looked lovely. She is a tall, handsome girl, though
too long-nosed and strong-jawed for beauty – takes after her
grandmother. She was studying when she and Thomas fell in
love. Dad said she must choose, either study or marry him,
but no carrying on. She refused to stop seeing the boy, so he
burned all her books. Marriage à la mode.

Afterwards we joined the motorcade and drove down
through the village, tooting and honking. But declined

pressing invitations to join the wedding feast at Danilia (The Corfu Experience, with thousand-seat taverna) and went to Papiri in town for Costa's home cooking. He was unable to find change for 5,000 drachmas, and put it on the slate.

Sunday, 28 May As we were breakfasting in pyjamas, old Vasili appeared with the promised branch from the orange tree we had admired, to give us a graft. He grafted three slips on the freak, thorny Ur-citrus by the drive. A neat job. Complains that his knees are too stiff for him to manage more than one tree at a time, and that his hands are getting shaky, but 'once upon a time how I used to graft!'.

We met the Manessis at Benitses, equipped for a picnic, and decided to head for one of the beaches behind Ay. Mathia. Took the wrong track and wandered about in olive groves of immeasurable age, brilliant with patches of corn marigold, scarlet poppies and blue Venus's looking-glass. Nets everywhere with olives on them, parties of harvesters, and bulging sacks waiting for collection, and still there are trees covered with shiny black fruit. Goodness knows when this year's harvest will be done. At one dead end George got a net wrapped round his front wheel. What with this and much conversation with the pickers – one of whom, as usual, George knew – it was half past two before we ate our picnic, still under the trees. Eventually we came out among vineyards and peach orchards and black-headed buntings singing from telephone wires, and so down to a windy shore covered with seaweed, which we spurned, and came back for a splendid swim at St John of the Pigeons at five in the afternoon. The day so lovely, the country so beautiful, and the company so good that none of us minded the ridiculous drive.

At home, Spiro the Father-in-Law brought mulberries and loquats, and we drank ouzo. Daisy rang. She is not well and is going to London. Angelo, her brother, says she has lung cancer. All those fags.

Wednesday, 31 May Very damp morning and overcast all day with occasional showers, Went for a *coupa* – drinks–cum–buffet lunch – given by Georgetto Theotoki at his Ropa estate, where he grows and makes his well-known wine. The usual hard-core Corfiot mob. Profuse and excellent food and drink, and, like all Georgetto's parties, extremely noisy and jolly.

After a heavy *bizolo* (the Corfiot siesta) I needed exercise and climbed to the top of Ay. Kyriaki. The little church seems in as much need of repair as last year, but at least the roof hasn't collapsed. The hillside was alive with activity. I met old Vasili's son-in-law, the schoolmaster, coming down on his motor-bike, wearing his khaki outfit, with matching ear-flap cap and accompanying a truck laden with sacks of olives. Another of our neighbours was sitting under the trees with a friend sorting the fruit. Hector the baker's wife, Helen, was also working in a garden. Coming down, I came on a crone picking olives off the track. 'Still gathering, eh?' I said, with the traditional statement of the obvious. She regarded me sourly. 'What we peasants have to put up with in order to eat.' A justifiable comment twenty years ago. Olga used to take wild flowers to town, and sell them to buy bread for his children. But tourism has transformed all that. The village is full of cars, and schoolboys dash about on motor-cycles. Last year, photographing the church, I could not get fewer than four TV aerials into the picture. Yet folk memories rankle. It was no accident that in the 60s Corfu, the old feudal island, had the highest Communist vote in all Greece. The other day M. got a left-wing harangue from a taxi driver. Thank God, he said, he no longer had to call his fares, 'Sior Tony' or 'Sior Piero' – a form of address which died out long before he was born.

Friday, 2 June At 7.30, as we were pottering in the garden and contemplating a supper of boiled artichokes, our new friend Tryphon, the Anatolian Greek from London, rang and asked himself for a drink. By 9.15, and the third ouzo, he clearly didn't want to go, and accepted with alacrity the suggestion of eating in town, at Papiri's little taverna, which he didn't know. We drove down in his big car, ate veal with rice, drank a litre of retsina, and developed a great *kefi*. By the end we were agreed that the Greeks are the best, the only real, people.

Thursday, 8 June Ascension Day Learned that Daisy has lung cancer and is to be operated on Monday. M. rang her in London and found her, as one would expect, rational and composed.

Saturday, 10 June Joined up with the Ricketts and their friend Josie Baird for lunch at the Nychterida, where we met Elizabeth Glenconner. Had the place to ourselves and ate well, under the pergola. The three ladies all wore large straw hats – I don't think I have ever seen Elizabeth without one, and Pauline seldom. Denis, the old scholar, quoted bits of Euripides, and P.J. and I swapped chunks of English poetry, and we felt jolly and civilised.

On the way home we stopped at Kokkini, Maria's parents' house on the old Skevophylaka estate, where Maria had suggested we gather apricots. Gerasimos the caretaker appeared. We identified ourselves, and he thereafter called M. 'my gold'. He picked a basketful from the trees and raided the henhouse for a dozen eggs.

The swallows have finally deserted the nest. To compensate, a family of great tits, reared in a crevice of the garden wall, emerged with much fuss and self-importance. The young sat in a row on top of the wall and then one by one made their maiden flights, first to the roof and then away into the olives.

Monday, 12 June Daisy was operated on today. First reports are hopeful. S, the Father-in-Law came very early to cut undergrowth on the slope. He did a good morning's work and then ate a dozen *keftedes*, bread and about half a pound of cheese, and drank most of a bottle of wine (having earlier refreshed himself with coffee and *tsipouro*). He told me that he had a very large *koupa* at the Thin One's last night, was incapable of riding his scooter, and got home at 12.30, falling down three times en route.

Tuesday, 13 June All swam at A.Y., where we heard the first cicada. Weather threatening rain. Nightingales were singing at bed-time.

Friday, 16 June Flew over thick cloud, golden in the setting sun, and came down to a dusky Athens. Faithful Kyr Vasili there to meet us with a trolley. Lights and fireworks marked a Pasok rally in Central Athens, in preparation for the election on Sunday. Nothing in the papers but partisan bragging and blackguarding.

Ina not looking too bad. Had a light supper and sank gratefully into the old double bed.

9

Aspects of a City: Constantinople

Europeans visit Turkey for all sorts of reasons. Romantic philhellenes itch to stand above the walls of windy Troy, where Helen once drew men's eyes to her as she passed, or to share with the darting lizards the warm steps of Ionian stoas and temples. Devout Christians trace the footsteps of the Apostle Paul, or, if profound connoisseurs of the psyche, seek out the rock churches and cells of Cappadocia and ponder the extravagances of mysticism. There are also the fanatics for high and far-off lands, drawn to the empty Anatolian plateau and the ancient home of the Armenians before they were massacred by the Turks. These go to Lake Van and the upper waters of the Euphrates, where they can smell Asia stretching away and beyond from the Caspian to the China Sea. (There are an increasing number who go simply to lie on the southern beaches, but that is less a reason than a symptom of the creeping viral infection of tourism.)

Most serious travellers will try, sooner or later, to set eyes on the imperial city between the Golden Horn and the sea of Marmara, the domes and minarets of its profile, the courts and pavilions of the Topkapi Saray, the shameless richness of the sultans' jewels and porcelain, and the windowless labyrinth of lust and boredom where they kept their women. A certain number of Greeks even make the journey. Most Greeks, for sound historico-psychological reasons, do not take holidays in Turkey, but there are those who feel impelled to go on pilgrimage, half religious to the central shrine of Orthodoxy, half nostalgic to the heart of the empire once deemed to be the earthly simulacrum of the kingdom of heaven.

No Greek goes, as the rest of us do, to Istanbul. He does not speak, even in travel literature, of going to Istanbul. He goes to Constantinople, the city of Constantine, or simply to the City, and what he means is clear to everyone. To talk of going to Istanbul is a solecism, since the name is no more than a Turkish corruption of 'Eis tin polin', that is, 'to the city'.

It was in that spirit that we flew from Athens by Turkish Airlines. For me, a mere associate member of the world-wide Hellenic club, the pilgrimage lacked its full emotional involvement, but many years of desultory reading in and around Byzantine history and culture had left me anxious to discover what physical traces were still to be found. I wondered, in particular, whether the City carried any qualities of 'Greekness' capable of evoking a response from a visitor homesick for his Hellenic past.

After five centuries of obliteration, one could not expect to find much remaining of the medieval city. The results of my observations, nevertheless, were more negative than I had hoped. For a start, the landscape and the atmosphere neither look nor feel Greek. The air is damp and northern. The light has none of the Aegean sharpness and intensity. The entry to the Bosporus, with its opaque, celadon-green water and the bridge to Asia materialising from a pearly mist, beguiles the eye, but speaks not of the Mediterranean but of the Black Sea, and of sources in the Danube and the slow rivers of Russia.

Nor is there any significant trace of classical Greece. The acropolis and temples of Byzas's city have vanished, demolished or buried beneath the palace and gardens of Seraglio Point. What remains of secular building from pre-Ottoman times is Roman in design and execution, the vestiges of the new capital city of the Roman Empire, its pompous strength symbolic of the orientalised despotism which the state had become by Constantine's time.

Travellers agree that the city should be seen for the first

time from the waters of the Propontis, but there is a stirring moment in the approach by land from the west. Seem-
ingly endless and soulless housing estates at last give way to
older and more haphazard building. Glimpses of the Marmara shore begin to appear on the right hand. Then, suddenly, the Theodosian walls swoop down the hillside, and
you are entering close by the Golden Gate through which the
emperors used to return after triumph in battle.

The aqueduct of Valens – distant cousin of the Pont du
Gard – and the vast underground cisterns are fine works of
Roman engineering, but the land walls have an extra touch
of exhilaration. In themselves walls are boring. Once you
have seen a hundred yards of Hadrian's Wall, or of the Great
Wall of China, you have seen the lot. Their appeal is the
knowledge that for centuries men stood on them and looked,
with civilisation behind them, towards the frustrated barbarians outside. So it was on the walls of Constantinople for a
thousand years. For the Byzantines civilisation was co-ter-
minous with the realm of emperor and Patriarch, no matter
how many German pretenders might call themselves holy
and Roman.

It is particularly poignant to stand on the walls' highest
point, near the Adrianople Gate and to imagine the sight of
Sultan Mehmet's besieging host encamped below, and the
roar of the huge cannon as it hurled another monstrous ball
against the crumbling battlements. Here finally the defences
were scaled and the last Constantine flung himself into the
fray, and was lost for ever with his city.

The Theodosian walls end some distance from the Golden
Horn. The last section at the north end was replaced, at the
time of the Comneni, by a new wall which made a wide arc
to include the Shrine of Blachernae and the adjacent palace.
The later emperors resided there in preference to the old
palace beside the Hippodrome, which was allowed to fall
into decay. They also built, near the junction of the old and
new walls, a third palace, that of the Prophyrogeniton – that

is, of princes born during their father's reign in the Por-
phyry Chamber. After the Ottoman conquest it was used as
an imperial menagerie and housed elephants and giraffes. In
the seventeenth century the animals were removed, and the
palace was for a time a brothel. This was replaced by a pot-
tery of some renown and later (such was the versatility of
Turkish disdain) by a hospital for Jewish paupers. In the end
the roof fell in and the whole building collapsed except for
the three-storey inner courtyard wall, which is still known as
the Palace of the Sovereign, Tekfur Saray.

The wall, with brick courses traversing the masonry and
its marble window frames, is the sole surviving piece of
domestic Byzantine architecture which is more than frag-
mentary. It is listed as an ancient monument. A notice at the
gate to the area – which lies between the inner and outer land
walls – declared the site to be open to the public on Monday,
Thursday and Sunday. It being a Turkish Saturday, the gate
was not locked and we went in. The courtyard is now
covered with ill-kept grass and is surrounded on three sides
by ruins. In its centre stood a small shack, outside which a
man was lying asleep in the sun on a low bed. A dumpy
woman in the shapeless garments and head scarf of an
Anatolian peasant emerged from the hut, holding a grubby
booklet, and indicated by signs that we must each pay her
2,000 Turkish liras (about 30p). There were no signs or
information of any kind. So much for imperial Byzantium.

That left ecclesiastical Constantinople. Many churches
have been Islamified, and the ancient basilica of St Irene was
shut, for undisclosed reasons. We visited three, perhaps the
most important, and each significant in a different way.

The great church of the Holy Wisdom, Ayia Sophia, was
dejected and dejecting, like a huge stranded hulk. The interior was partly filled, to the roof, with scaffolding. This made
it difficult to appreciate fully the stupendous achievement
of Anthemius's dome. In my own case, I must confess, ad-
miration is tempered by a distaste for very large places of

worship. Ayia Sophia seems to me to suffer from the Roman love of size for its own sake. (In St Peter's they show you a line on the floor marking the point to which the west of St Paul's in London would reach if it were put inside their cathedral, as though piety was measured by the cubic metre.) Worse still was the feeling that a holy place had been insulted, not only by being stripped of its decoration and sacred pictures, or even by having been used as a mosque, but principally because as a 'museum' it is being treated as unfit to serve either Christian or Moslem. We left angry and ashamed.

The Oecumenical Patriarchate is still a Christian centre, but is disheartening in a different way. The church and its attendant buildings lurk unobtrusively in the run-down district of Fener, named from the old Phanari or lighthouse on the Golden Horn. It showed little sign of activity. The Patriarch had gone to Switzerland for his health. Of the forty or so priests said to be attached to the church there was no evidence. The only other people in the church were its guardians, two gentle, middle-aged laymen. They were, they told us, refugees from the island of Imbros, now Turkish Imruz. They were pleased to see visitors, lit candles for us at a lamp before an icon, and showed us the modest treasures. It gives the impression of surviving on sufferance, by keeping a low profile – as indeed it has done ever since 1453. Folly to invite martyrdom by proclaiming the faith with processions and the ringing of bells. If history is anything to go by, the result would be the execution of the Patriarch, the burning down of the church, and the expulsion from Constantinople of its remaining Greek inhabitants. The present situation is, all the same, inglorious.

Redemption and a lifting of the spirit came at the third point of call, the church known as St Saviour in Chora, a little way below Tekfur Saray. Built in the eleventh and twelfth centuries, it was enlarged to its present form, and lavishly embellished about 1320 by Theodore Metochites, Grand

Logothete of the Empire under Andronicus II Paleologos. The names of the artists in mosaic and fresco painting employed by Metochites are unknown to us, but they must have been among the most brilliant of the late-Byzantine revival. The church became the Kariye mosque and most of the interior adornment was concealed by plaster. It was damaged by earthquakes, and fell into disuse. Only after 1948, when restoration was begun by the Byzantine Institute of America, was it discovered that, as if by a miracle, almost all the mosaics and frescoes were intact. They include some of the most powerful and inspired religious art that exists, culminating in an astonishing Anastasis. Christ is depicted rising from the dead into the sky like a dancer, and drawing up with him by either hand Adam and Eve, his fallen creation.

The Chora church is a 'museum' but the emotion of its murals is so intense that, unlike Ayia Sophia, it feels like a working church. I believed that I had at last found Byzantium, the city where at one time it was said that if you asked the price of a loaf the baker would ask you if you thought that the First Person of the Trinity was greater than the Second. For better or worse its values are not ours, in Britain or in Greece.

10

Aspects of a City: Istanbul

Over *yoghurtlu kepap* at the Divani Hotel, we fell into conversation with a solitary diner at the next table, a Dutchman in Istanbul on chewing-gum business. I ventured to say that I had seen little sign of the habit around the city, but he assured us that within twenty years the Turks would all be chewing and expectorating like World Series baseball players. He was, of course, simply reviving an old trade. The masticha trees of Chios for centuries provided gum for the women of the sultan's harem, one of whose more innocent pastimes was mastication. Now, however, Chinese pine trees yield the resin which gives the modern product its chewiness, and in which our friend was a dealer. (For that matter, if you buy a Greek straw hat from actual straw, not from plastic, it will have been made by the Chinese, who also fashion most of the hatchets to be found in Corfiot hardware shops.)

The resin-merchant told us that he knew no more honest businessman than the Turk. In the phrase of which the English were once able to be proud, a Turk's word is his bond. Our own short experience in shops, restaurants and even the Bazaars tended to confirm this. There was never a feeling of being got the better of. The straightforwardness, moreover, was matched by a friendly and helpful courtesy. This came as a relief. Greeks are apt to expect the worst from their old enemy. (Kyr Vasili, our Athenian taxi driver, used to quote the old saying that the Turks are polite barbarians, while the Greeks are civilised but rude.) Some philhellenes have spread the calumny that Turkish conversation is restricted to an unsmiling reiteration of the negative 'Yok'.

We made our way from Tekfur Saray to the Patriarchate on foot, reaching the Golden Horn at the old Hebrew quarter of Balat (from the Greek Palati, the Palace of Blachernae). The path led steeply down past the hovels of some of the worst slums in Europe. The inhabitants gave us directions with ready and dignified civility, and one man insisted on accompanying us for the last quarter-mile, to ensure that we did not miss our way. We then picked up a taxi, which we discovered to be operating illegally, when the driver asked us to alight half a block short of our destination in case the police saw him carrying passengers. Before lunching at Pandelis, the Greek restaurant in the gatehouse of the Egyptian spice market, we drank tea from tulip glasses, under the trees of an open-air café. The customers were all men, many with an indefinable air of eccentricity. I took the opportunity to show off the few words of Basic Turkish which I had memorised for the expedition. This produced approving smiles and nods from the surrounding tables, and for my *pièce de résistance*, 'ne güzel!' (how lovely!) a short round of applause.

On top of this pervasive goodwill, we were helped by a fortunate relationship with our dragoman. In order to reduce the problems of transport and language in a strange city, we had swallowed our prejudice against being bussed around as part of a tourist group, and had paid for a package holiday, with guide. On arrival at the airport we found that the package consisted of ourselves, a minibus driven by the pleasant and reliable Ismail, and our personal guide, a young man named Taner. He was still a trainee, and we came to suspect that we had been allotted to him because his English was doubtfully adequate for coping with a large flock. At times it bordered on the bizarre. Peculiarly baffling was the word 'priced' at intervals in his discourses, until we realised that this was his version of 'priest' – a term which he applied, with abandon, to every class of cleric, from patriarch to imam.

The minibus collected us punctually each morning, and Taner was our intimate companion for the next six or seven hours. To him the history of the city appeared to start in 1453, when it became Turkish by Mehmet II's conquest (of which he spoke with reverence), and most of his information thereafter was set out in better order and accuracy in the Blue Guide. He sprayed us with a shower of easily forgettable facts, such as the number of tonnes and cubic metres of steel in the two Bosporus bridges. But he was a nice boy. With no other tourists to consider, we were able when necessary to dictate what we did or did not want to see, and for how long. Taner took it all in good part, and was always willing to stand us a coffee, or a glass of the chilled yoghurt drink called *ayran*.

We learned many things about our guide, some more credible than others. He had served in the Turkish navy for eight years and had risen, he said, to the command of a vessel – a very small one, we suspected, for anybody looking less like a retired naval officer than Taner would have been hard to imagine. His subsequent venture into the tourist industry had brought him romance, in the form of a Finnish girl (neither very young nor very beautiful) whose snapshot he showed us from his wallet. During a fortnight's holiday a few months before, she had found love and an offer of marriage. They had not seen each other since, but Taner was confident about their future together. His highest, hidden ambition, however, was to join his cousin as a baritone with the Turkish State Opera.

Whatever the wonders of his mental world, he showed sound taste in Moslem architecture. On the first morning, profiting by the elasticity of our arrangements, he announced that we would start with an unscheduled visit to the Süleymaniye mosque. The greatest building in all Istanbul, he declared, and he was right. The Blue Mosque of Sultan Ahmet is a glorious effervescence, a baroque organ toccata of domes, domelets and semi-domes; the austere majesty of the Süleymaniye represents the awesome, all-encompassing Oneness of God, as apprehended and interpreted by the genius of one of his supreme artists, Süleyman's architect Sinan. Serenity and dignity pervade the whole complex, which includes the tombs of the Sultan himself and his beloved Roxelana, and a surprise small graveyard full of purple hollyhocks, overtopping the grey turbans of the slender tombstones.

It was the more pleasing for us to remember – and we said nothing of it to Taner – that Sinan was Greek by birth, and was converted to Islam after being caught by a *devsirme*, or *paedomazoma*, one of the regular levies of Christian youths for a life in the Sultan's service. Thus, by a twist of fortune he ended by rivalling Anthemius who designed Ayia Sophia, and becoming the peer of Wren and Bernini in the history of architecture. He was also a senior contemporary of another exile from the Greek world, El Greco.

We had hoped for a hotel in the old city, but lost nothing by being lodged at the Divani, at the top of Pera, across the Golden Horn. Old-fashioned, it offered nostalgic standards of style and service. The capacious lifts of massive construction bore one upwards with reassuring deliberation. Our sultanic bed was matched by a cast-iron bath like an imperial horse-trough. The staff were numerous, efficient and friendly, from the waiter in full kit with black tie who delivered breakfast, to the small regiment of every rank, from mâitre down to long white-aproned table boys, in the excellent restaurant. The basement was given over to a large hairdressing, manicure and massage department. This was heavily patronised and appeared to perform the same social function, as a meeting place for gossip, as did the *hammam* inthe old days. A pianist in the café-bar and a string trio in the palm lounge dispensed romantic melodies from shows of the twenties.

We were staying in a relatively prosperous quarter, yet from our window we regularly saw, in a small park between us and the more modern Sheraton, two gipsies with performing bears. Crippled or mutilated beggars were common in the streets, while Taksim Square was the territory of small shoeshine boys, more numerous and importunate than any I had seen since the Athens of 1945. The dinginess, and the general lack of dignity, of Istanbul's secular buildings were depressingly unworthy of the ecclesiastical architecture, both Byzantine and Ottoman, of which they formed the setting. Even the Grand Bazaar, with its maze of narrow shop-lined lanes, is so modernised that it has all but lost the Oriental flavour which used to spice the adventure of being relieved of one's money.

We made an excursion from the hotel down Istiklal Avenue to buy *loukoum* (Turkish delight), for a private family reason. When Marily's grandmother was a small girl, she accompanied her father Dimitri Ralli, then prime minister of Greece, on an official visit to the Sublime Porte. Because she was so young she was permitted to attend the all-male divan at which Sultan Abdul Hamid received her father in audience. The Sultan asked her what she would like best for a present. She replied, a pillow, please, made of *loukoum*, which she could lick before going to sleep. A command went forth to Hadji Bekir, official *loukoumier* to the palace, and a block of *loukoum* was delivered the same evening to the hotel. A hundred years later we found the shop of Hadji Bekir and bought a box of delight in memoriam.

Excursions outside the City gave us two relaxed and pleasurable days. On Friday Taner escorted us up the Bosporus on the ferry which zig-zags between a succession of small towns, along the well-wooded shores. Summer palaces and country houses contrast with the twin castles – Rumeli Hisar on the European bank, Anadolu Hisar on the Asian – with which Mehmet strangled the City to death. The boat was full and carried many vendors of food drink and trinkets. At Kanlica a seller of the local yoghurt came aboard, justifying its reputation of being the best in the world.

At Sariyer we asked Taner if the imam's call to prayer was heard in Turkey. He pooh-poohed the idea, but in an open place near our restaurant a large group of men, inmates of an old people's home, were on their knees for the midday Friday prayers. On the day before, in the Topkapi Saray, we had noted many devout visitors to a building where relics of the Prophet are preserved.

Sariyer, some seven miles from the entrance to the Black Sea, was as close as we got to the ancient world of the Greek colonies which ringed the Euxine and extended up the Danube and as far north as Rostov on the Don. Ismail met us and drove us back to the city. En route we crossed the first Bosporus bridge to Beylerbey, on the eastern shore. We detected a note of pride in Taner's voice when he proclaimed, 'Now we are in Asia!' He himself had been born, and still lived, in Kadiköy (ancient Chalcedon) on the Asiatic side. One suspects that all Turks know themselves to be incongruous applicants for membership of the European Community, for their roots – and perhaps their souls too – are in Central Asia from where both Seljuks and Ottomans came, and where so many of their kinsmen still abide.

The second voyage, on our last day, was across the Propontis for some thirty kilometres, to the Princes' Islands, so-called because of the number of deposed emperors and their families who were sent there, to pass their years of exile among the monasteries. During the nineteenth century, when travelling to the islands became easier, many wealthy Greeks and Armenians, and a smaller number of Turks, built houses, particularly on Prinkipo, or Büyükada, the farthest and largest of the group. They also became popular holiday resorts.

We travelled on one of the regular ferries, crowded with Sunday trippers. They were predominantly young male and noisy, but not rowdy. One group on deck made Oriental music on drum, accordion and voice, to which others danced, in a style like the Greek but lacking its distinctive controlled fluidity. One young man executed a spectacular belly-dance. Our nearest companions were a serious naval cadet officer in spotless whites, a young couple with three beautiful small children, and a trio of two lean, predatory young men and a much younger pretty boy, whom they subjected to constant banter and horseplay, combined with fondling and stroking. They appeared to be bound for a Sunday of secluded sodomy.

Both the harbour and the surrounding country on Prinkipo were more Greek in look and atmosphere than anything we had seen on the mainland. We ate on the waterfront, bought white apricots at the street market, and drove a little way out of town in a two-horse phaeton, the only form of wheeled transport, except bicycles, allowed on the island. At the more picturesque wooded spots, many families were picnicking on the ground – a habit, Taner said, to which the Turks are given. The return voyage was marginally quieter than the morning, and ended with the classic approach by water to the city, the silhouette of Seraglio Point and the domes of Ayia Sophia and the Blue Mosque almost black against a dusty golden sky.

The last two days gave us two separate glimpses of the collective Turkish character. On Friday morning, before we set off on our own for the Land Walls, we were told that at two o'clock there was to be a demonstration in Pera, against the current Bulgarian treatment of the Turkish minority. When we returned, at about five, platoons of young men were still marching through the streets, in military formation, punching the air with clenched fists and chanting anti-Bulgarian slogans. The tail of the procession, when it eventually passed our hotel, was rounded off by a company of fully armed police.

Coming back from our island trip, we found the main road through Pera given over entirely to a stream of cars which continued for the next two hours. The occupants were all blowing their horns, shouting and singing, and waving blue flags from the windows. It was not a political demonstration. They were not celebrating the conquest of the City, an Armenian massacre, or victory over the Bulgars. Their football team had just won a game.

We could not help remembering Kyr Vasili.

At the Centre

After a meal of such diverse flavours – Roman, Byzantine, Pontic, Ottoman – it was imperative to clear the palate with a cold draught from the springs of Hellas. Our gentle, green Corfu was too far on the fringe (to Greece rather as the Hebrides are to Scotland), too Italianate, too soft in outlines and in climate for our purpose. Not for the first time, we needed the Aegean and its islands, Socrates' Greek frogpond, for a cleansing of the spirit.

The Cyclades are the centre of the Aegean, and the uninhabited isle of Delos lies at the heart of the Cyclades. It is, by influences of legend, magic and history, unique among islands in Hellenic folk-memory. The myth goes that Poseidon first called it from the deep with his trident, and that it was a floating island, altering its position in the sea. When Leto, the Titan's daughter, became pregnant by Zeus, jealous Hera persecuted her and drove her from place to place to prevent her from giving birth. Zeus enabled her to fly to the island in the form of a quail (the old name for Delos was Ortygia, meaning Quail-island). He also anchored the island to the sea-bed with adamantine chains. Restored to woman's form, and leaning against a palm-tree, Leto then gave birth to Apollo the sun-god, and to Artemis the moon-goddess.

Delos is known to have been held in the utmost sanctity from the start of Greek history. It was purified by a special ceremony, and neither birth nor death was permitted to defile it, the parturient and the dying being transferred to a nearby island. Religious rites of high solemnity, in honour of Apollo, were celebrated annually and attended by deputations from all over the Greek world. Quinquennial games were also held. There was a large temple to Apollo, as well as a smaller one of Artemis, with an adjoining precinct, and a sacred lake where the birth was said to have taken place.

The treasury of the alliance against Persia in the fifth century B.C., known as the Confederacy of Delos, was situated on the island. In post-classical times, and throughout the Roman Empire, Delos became prosperous as a port and mercantile centre, with a town of fine houses, and a theatre, on the hill above the old religious complex. Because of its holiness it was never attacked or molested. Only with the decline of the Empire was it deserted and left open to pirates and Saracens. Earthquakes and the Mykoniots completed its destruction.

Neither Marily nor I had ever been to Delos. Now seemed the ideal time to repair that failure. Travellers, other than shining ones on Swan Hellenic cruises, reach Delos by caique from Mykonos. We determined to spend a few nights there, ignoring warnings that we would be exposed to transvestites and other assorted deviants. Mykonos is served from Athens by small aeroplanes, but it seemed more therapeutic and respectful of its insularity to take the boat from Piraeus.

The taxi collected us from the Psychiko house at 6 a.m. We drove swiftly to the port through quiet streets. (In spite of Athens's modern size and brashness, the journey, with its morning-sharp glimpses of the Parthenon, was not very different from the army jeep-ride to catch the sailing *kaiki*, *Ay. Nikolaos*, for Paros on my first ever Aegean journey. We bought fresh warm *koulouria* from the eternal quayside vendor, took them aboard the *Panayia Tinou*, ordered *kafedakia* from the first-class bar, and ate our breakfast on deck, surveying the scene.

The *Panayia* was a big new ship, named after the Virgin of the miraculous ikon of the great church of Tinos, our first port of call. She is famous for healing all over the Orthodox world, and many pilgrims come to the shrine to pray or give thanks. Since the introduction of the roll-on-and-off car ferries, the size and number of the inter-island boats have transformed the Piraeus of the battered, chummy steamers. Near us were four Cretan boats, *Aptera, Samaina, Phaistos* and *Ayia Galini*, as well as *Ialysos* (for Patmos and Rhodes), *Omiros* and the little orange-hulled *Naxos*. At seven, the first bells rang for the feast of SS Peter and Paul. We were upon the point of sailing, and the ship's first siren blast had sounded, when a coach came at speed along the quay and stopped with a jolt outside, to discharge a load of pilgrims from Macedonia bound for Tinos. They were hustled aboard with their baggage, and ten minutes late, to another clatter of church bells, we cast off. Outside port, we overhauled *Naxos* (presumably bound for her eponymous island) and set course for Cape Sounion.

There were few passengers. A spare cabin was available for the asking, and we retired to rest for an hour, emerging in time to see Poseidon's temple columns on the headland. A perfect Aegean morning, with only a light ripple. Between Dzia and Kythnos storm petrels fluttered in small flocks, escorted by Manx shearwaters. In the pervading midsummer light, tawny islands floated in an ink-dark sea. Andros to port and Syros to starboard swung up and were left behind. Our companions on deck were young male Japanese, two or three Dutch couples, and a hippyish American, with a bald dome and a short pony-tail, laboriously underlining passages in the *Christian News*. Tinos town, with its big ornate church, was a dazzle of white against rocky hills. The Macedonians and many others of the faithful, but not the Christian newsreader, disembarked, and we left on the last leg to Mykonos. In the strait, two sportive dolphins bestowed good fortune on our venture. We docked exactly five hours after leaving the Piraeus.

Many citizens were offering rooms, but we had booked in advance. An elderly man with an open tricycle-van offered to convey us and luggage to the hotel. Marily climbed in

behind with the bags, I up the front, and we rattled spank-
ingly through the narrow flagged alleys which pass for streets
in Mykonos town. The Kounenis hotel lay in the district –
just outside the densely built town centre – known as the
Tria Pighadia, the Three Wells, full of gardens shaded by tall
trees. The hotel itself, though simple in the old island style,
had modern comforts. Our room had a stable-type door
opening on to one of a number of gardens, criss-crossed
by paths of whitewash-edged flagstones, which formed a
secluded square within the surrounding houses. We looked
out on a small lemon grove, cypresses, hibiscus and mag-
nolia, blazing patches of sunflower and a clump of tall yellow
lilies. There were also a pergola laden with heavy bunches
of grapes and a row of hanging gourds. The fauna of
Eden consisted of hens, cats, a corkscrew-tailed dog of in-
decipherable ancestry, and two very loud parakeets in cages.

Mykonos town, famous in postcards for its windmills and
Petros the pelican, in fact represents the best, and least
corrupted, of Cycladean domestic architecture. The starkness
of its cubes and rectangles has been softened by layer upon
layer of whitewash, decorative detail is rare and restrained,
while the potential monotony of the white is relieved, spar-
ingly, by areas of bright blue and ochreous red, from natural
pigments. We were impressed, walking in the town that first
evening, by the success of the authorities (who put Corfu to
shame) in controlling Greek constructional extravagance,
and maintaining traditional standards, in spite of the fact that
almost every house had become either a bar or a boutique.
The colours are regularly refreshed, and all householders
are obliged to sweep and wash the roadway in front of
their establishments each morning. By ten o'clock no trace
remains of last night's Vanity Fair.

We visited Delos on the first of July, which is kept by
the Orthodox as the Feast of the Incorruptibles, the medical
saints Cosmas and Damian. They are, or were, the patron
saints of physicians. Fishermen however – or at least those of

Mykonos – also come under their protection. On the evening before, we found a large area of the waterfront covered by stands of glowing charcoal for grilling, and by wood fires over which enormous caldrons of water were being heated for the preparation of the fish soup known as *kakavia*. Outside a small church three musicians, seated on the ground, played the plaintive folk melodies of the Cyclades on accordion, drum and an ur-bagpipe made from a whole sheep's carcase. By nightfall, the place was thronged with foreigners, mostly blatant heterosexuals, to whom soup, grilled fish and wine from the barrel were distributed, free.

In the morning, a cats' chorus woke us for the early boat to Delos. The tickets were issued by a grave man with a neat grizzled beard and a dark blue baseball cap, inscribed in white with the crest and motto of the University of Oxford. The young skipper of the *kaiki Neraida II* was himself wildly bearded, to match his exuberant black curls. What could be seen of his face bore signs of debauchery and fatigue from the night's festivities. The voyage to Delos lasted half an hour, and was calm.

Theodore Bent, writing of his visit to Delos in 1885, describes the state of the ruins as a scene of 'desolation and destruction perhaps more complete than that of Nineveh. . . All round stretches a vast sea of ruins, recalling Pompeii in extent and complete annihilation.' Some restoration has been done on the post-classical town, but the ancient temple and santuary looked much as they did a century ago. The temple is practically level with the ground. The Sacred Lake has dried up and is now a thicket of reeds. In the sanctuary, two details caught the imagination: a gatepost of a Dionysiac shrine, surmounted by half of a giant marble phallus; and the sixth-century Minoa fountain. This was a square pool with steps leading down into opaque green water, in which little fish wiggled and emerald frogs goggled.

The well-paved streets and market place of the Hellenistic town, with its cisterns and the houses built round courts with well-preserved mosaics, conjured up the equivalent of a busy small cathedral city with a decent theatre. We climbed to the top of the auditorium and photographed each other, wearing the Chinese straw sun hats we had bought in Mykonos. Grasshoppers chirped among the hot grey rocks, the pale barley grass whispered in the wind, and the indigo sea was restless with white horses. The place was not numinous at all, but it was utterly and inescapably Greek.

The return voyage was made in the teeth of a sudden strong *meltemi*, the summer wind of the Aegean. Spray broke over the gunwales, making our lips salt. We lunched late, and well, at Antonini's. Life mulled round us. Light, light, light – the retsina-flavoured noontide Greece of the mind's eye, to which Constantinople and Corfu are both peripheral.

12

Ayia Kyriaki, 1970

Since you cannot be certain whether your journey is to last for ever or only for a day, it is well to start very early in the morning, while it is yet dark, with sleep and the sweet tang of coffee heavy on the tongue. So you will be in time – pausing at a turn in the path where the bell's yammer is deadened by the shoulder of the hill – to see the sunrise spilled out golden as truth on the face of the water to lead tired fishermen home. And you will also be in time to join the people of God, that is to say the butcher, the baker, members of the silver band, and the white-kerchiefed women who gossip on doorsteps in the evening, in a high dwelling-place, holy and humble as a stable, with candles in their hands and bay-leaves under their feet, lifting up Alleluias among the Cherubim. And afterwards there will still be time to pick mountain herbs, sharp as nostalgia, as you come down eating the bread of your joy and gladness. You will have this to remember, though your journey last for thirty years, or for ever.

13

Ayia Kyriaki, 1989

We got back to Corfu just in time to make the ascent, once again, for our special saint's yearly remembrance. We met Irene at Pahatika, and she led us up by a path we had not known of, on the west side of the hill. The Ten Saints were pink in the first sunlight across the valley, but we missed the golden roadway on the face of the gulf. (In any case, the old path, with the empress's steps, had been needlessly blocked by a new house, and nobody climbed that way any more.)

The journey had been going on now for ten years. They had not been kind to the little church. The roof let in the sky at several points, the doors were sagging on their hinges, and much of the interior wood seemed in danger of disintegrating. Also, the separate belfry had been split and partly demolished by lightning. A couple of years before, bustling Papa Thanasi had goaded his flock into transporting roofing sheets to the top of the hill, by making each worshipper carry one sheet on his or her head on the day of the annual service, like an army of umbrella ants. The sheets had lain in neat stacks ever since. Talk at Hector's shop often came round to the deplorable state of the church. It was always made, obliquely and charmingly, crystal clear that the repairs were a Bulgari concern, always had been, and always would be. As my father-in-law had at one time done some restoration and marked the occasion with a marble plaque honouring Kyriaki as the protectress of his family, perhaps he had only himself to blame.

The villagers straggled, panting, in twos and threes over

the last stony brow of the summit plateau. A few young had kept the traditional all-night vigil round the church. Papa Spiro kept us all waiting till eight o'clock. This would not have happened in Papa Thanasi's day, nor in old Papa Pipi's. Both liked to be there first, to keep everything right and hear late confessions. Most of our own neighbours were there, and of course Mantou, now seventy-five, and Gerasimos the psaltis, eighty-four with a gammy leg. The *proedros*'s wife had brought her two young sons (who took communion in embarrassed prominence), and there was a small contingent, including a very positive psaltis, from Ayious Deka, a much more pious village than ours. After service, Taki's lads received general congratulations and good wishes, and there was a feeling that the village was secure for another year.

The little saint looked at us from her icon, we thought, with reproach, sharpened by the fact that she had, as we knew, a working church, in good order, in Mykonos, and a full-time priest to ring a passing-bell for departed parishioners. Marily promised her that she would really do something about the roof.

14

Kalokairi

The modern Greek names for the seasons of the year form an example of the continuity of the language over about 3,000 years. *Himonas*, winter, has the longest and noblest pedigree, having kept its form and meaning since the Homeric poems. It is related to *hion*, the word for snow, and, so the scholars say, is linked, through Sanskrit, to the Him- of the Himalayas. So it is the cold or snowy season. (The water melon is popularly known in Corfu as *to himoniko*, the wintry one, because of its refreshing coolness on a hot day.) *Phthinoporo*, literally 'the end of fruiting', has also been used as the name for autumn since classical times.

The ancient word for spring was *eär*, and does not seem to have been superseded by *anixi* until comparatively lately. But *anixi* – more correctly *anoixi* – has existed in its original meaning of 'opening' since the days of Thucydides. *Kalokairi*, the fair or lovely season, seems to have been a child of Byzantium, supplanting the ancient *theros* as the name of summer, though *kalokairia* had a classical usage as meaning a happy state of affairs. The *kalokairi* covers roughly the three months from mid-May till early September with a core of fierce and rain-less dominance during July and August, when sensible men suspend serious endeavour.

This lovely season began in a flurry of endeavour, in the shape of a parliamentary election. For weeks before we went to the City our Blues and Greens had been screaming slogans at each other through megaphones, and painting and overpainting dichromatic insults on wayside walls. It appeared that the voters' choice lay between thieving crypto-communists and murderous monarcho-fascists. PASOK were confident of victory, in spite of the taint of financial scandals. Any suggestion that massive corruption ill became the government of a noble nation, and a member of the European Community, was met with a shrug and the opinion that politicians are all the same. Mr Papandreou's infidelity, with a blonde former air hostess half his age, aroused a humorous envy of the old boy's continuing virility.

The election was held during our absence from Corfu, and ended with a majority of one seat for Constantine Mitsotakis and the New Democracy. Calm was restored to the village. For us, the change of government, after eight years, wrought a corresponding change in the attitude of the telephone authority, OTE. We at once got the phone for which we had petitioned for so long. We considered it prudent, all the same, not to tell them that we had by-passed officialdom by running a private party-line from brother Stephen's house over the garden wall.

Meanwhile Daisy was back in Athens. She had undergone a lung operation in London, and been given a hopeful prognosis. We persuaded her to come to us to convalesce. She was fragile and nervous. However, a few days of tranquillity on the terrace restored her strength and spirits. We swam at Alipa, and on her last evening we walked in a sunset of slanting gold up to the old empty village of Dafnata, from where you can see both seas, to the east the gulf and Epirus, to the west the Korissia lagoon and the open Ionian. Then the girls drove to the Tsaros for a chicken and chips take-away, while I watered the garden, and we ate it with a bottle of retsina, and were happy as in the old days, and hoped for the best.

High summer was slow in coming. The changeable spring weather continued, swinging between heavy days with distant grumbles of thunder and spells of brilliant north-westerly *maïstro*, making our terrace too draughty to sit out. Still, the sun imposed a pattern on the day. From ten till six it was too hot for exertion. Since the garden and flower-pots needed constant watering, this had to be done (loveliest time of all) around sunrise, or late in the evening. We also tried to swim before or after the midday heat. The beach we loved most was the small pebbly bay of Kodhraka, beyond Mesonghi, which is shaded by trees and has a ferny fresh-water spring behind the rocky point.

Most of the nearer beaches were overloaded with sun-beds, umbrellas, pedalos and oiled bodies, and restless with paragliding and jet-skis. But Ay. Yanni (Irene's St John of the Pigeons) was undeveloped and, at least till August, almost empty in the morning. Thick bushes of Vitex Agnus-castus* with long purple flower spikes grew a few feet from the sea's edge. These attracted two separate species of pied butterflies, as well as a variety of bees – a dapper fellow in black and white stripes, a smaller orange one, and several huge black bombers. One day we were surprised to see a shoal of little fishes swimming with their heads above the surface, submerging now and then to take in water.

At Kapoutsi we specialised in sunsets. At midsummer the sun rolled like a red-hot cannon ball down the slope of the mountain behind Peleka, stirring a half-hope that it would plunge with a hiss and a column of steam into the ocean. Sometimes, with luck, if the moon was very new and Venus an evening star, one could watch Aphrodite following Apollo to the rim of heaven, pursued by Artemis of the silver bow.

But the best hour was that of the morning watering. Nature, refreshed by the night, relished a respite before the sun's onslaught began. Nobody was stirring. Best of all there was no background noise. Shortly the cicadas, our *dzidzikes*, would start their racket and keep it up till sundown. The road

*Known in English as the chaste-tree. Its seeds look much like brown pepper-corns, and were used as seasoning by monks in lieu of real pepper, which was reputed to inflame carnal desire. Hence the plant's popular name of monk's pepper.

below us would provide a continual accompaniment of car horns and the roars and stutters of motor-cycles and scooters negotiating the steep bends, and the loudspeaker vans of the sellers of artichokes, courgettes, aubergines and water melons (according to the month), household utensils, plastic chairs, wine grapes and young turkeys.

After dark the *dzidzikes* were replaced by the crickets. These came in two varieties of voice. One ticked like a clock, the other made the sound of a high-pitched electric bell. They were difficult to locate by ear. One small ventriloquist had his home in the front porch, but I never could find him. The scops owls fluted lugubriously all night, while watchdogs on the properties round us could not refrain from answering each other back. At dawn all this became still, until Hussein in his stable heard me at work and called good morning, and the seven o'clock bus from town came grinding up the hill.

In July the Father-in-Law gave us several more days of his time, clearing thickets of broom and bramble, delivering a load of olive logs, splitting them with his monstrous axe, and stacking them in the store against the cold weather. Over the refreshments which fuelled these exertions, he revealed a tender soul behind his sardonic manner. He recalled all-night vigils on the Eve of Ayia Kyriaki with a romantic glint which suggested that religion had not been uppermost in his mind on the star-lit summit. He went on to inquire if my marriage had been a love-match, and nodded approvingly at the satisfactory reply. He also told us, apparently in all seriousness, an odd story of a snake, which fell into his well. He rescued it with a bucket, and it slithered off towards cover. But before disappearing it stopped, looked at him and made a little bow, as if to say thankyou.

In retrospect the August is a kaleidoscope of pictures for the family album – children swimming, or playing in the shallows, on the golden beaches of the south-west; children being given rides, and occasionally kicked, by Hussein; children gathering almonds from the giant tree by the potato patch;

children swinging and playing badminton under the olives, playing ping-pong or Scrabble on the terrace; suppers for a dozen at the long table laden with mounds of spaghetti, loaves of Hector's bread, melons, water melons and peaches. For five weeks Kapoutsi became what we had planned and hoped it could be, a home for all our family to enjoy: Katherine and her Jamie and their three, Laura, Peter and Guy; Amanda and her three, Ben, Chris and three year-old Emma, from Vancouver (where she had had to leave her Jamie). During the peak fortnight the house slept all nine of them, Marily and I escaping to the little basement flat, where we dispensed breakfast to one or two at a time, beneath the pergola of black, strawberry-flavoured Isabella grapes.

There was a renewing of old contacts. As usual, Marily's niece Christine had come from Versailles, with her French husband Olivier and their brood of four under-nines (plus one on the way), while George and Elena's daughter Agalis and her Rob had brought their first and much longed-for child, the infant Marcantonio Giustiniani. All this resulted, under Christine's indefatigable leadership, in day-long expeditions to distant remembered bays for sports and swimming, and for picnics.

Some of the picnics were celebratory. The Great Manessi Picnic at Skidi, on 8 August, was their contribution to our fortieth wedding anniversary, and took in Agalis's and Rob's thirteenth as well. The company totalled thirty-one. Gentle sea in the morning was succeeded by more exhilarating swimming after lunch, with wind-surfing. The food was in the highest Greek picnic tradition – *melidzanosalata*, *spanakopita*, *pastitsio*, cold meat with tomato and cucumber, cheese and fruit, helped down by ouzo; later in the afternoon, iced tea with *pastafrolla* and *baklavadakia*, plus an apple tart baked by Sophia, into which, neglecting to wear her glasses, she had put citric acid instead of sugar.

Skidi's narrow level strand, backed by a low cliff, was little known and as good as a private beach. Later on we used it for a barbecue, on Laura's thirteenth birthday. The cast of characters was the same, less Amanda and family, who had gone home to Canada. While Jamie and Olivier prepared a charcoal fire, the children dashed in and out of the sea in a golden blaze of sunset, and the rest whetted their appetites with ouzo and *meze*. The sun turned to orange and then a clear red, before being swallowed in haze. Supper in the gloaming round the fire consisted of marinated pork chops, baked potatoes, *souvlakia* and, of course, a large chocolate cake with candles. The sea became dully luminous, each wave of the slow swell rising in a darker line before turning over, from right to left, in a fringe of foam. No sooner had the last light gone, than a rising moon behind the cliff created a ghost dawn, in which the children darted with torches like demented fireflies. Agalis saw the scene as a Breughel painting. To me, the ring of young faces, lit from below by torch and candle flame, was life imitating Goya.

We drove back by the east coast road. Moraitika and Benitses, the quiet villages of memory, were graceless slums of sleaze and honky-tonk, perilous with swaggering bands of beery British youth, and murdering sleep with a cacophony of competing discos.

The anniversary celebrations were crowned by an evening party at Kapoutsi for about seventy. Almost half were family. Only the Count, too old, he said, for late nights, was missing. The others were all close to us, either as friends such as the Manessi and Zolota clans, or as neighbours – the Kamarelis complete with grandchildren, Spiro and Koula Bogdanou, Vasilo, old Kyria Anna, and Leonidas and Leni. Irene wore a festive village costume, and old Olga had decked herself in a bridal outfit, which included an elaborate headdress and a distaff with wool on it. The effect was unfortunate. When she later saw the photograph she giggled, 'What a funny-looking little old woman!'

Two roasting spits, each with a kid, had been on the go

over charcoal since five, one turned by Leonidas and the other by merry bald Niko from the village, who long ago used to compete with Marily at playing marbles. There was also a grill of hamburgers and chicken. Sophia had made spinach and courgette pies, and Christine brought luxurious desserts, which the neighbours supplemented with a cake of more than Oriental splendour.

The local contingent arrived first and sat in a formal row making polite conversation, but food and wine and obstreperous small boys soon gave the party momentum and a *kefi* which lasted the night. George Manessi teased the young with elementary magic tricks, and Olivier, amusing and inventive, devised a ceremonial climax. The children filed out of the olive grove beside the terrace, bearing a total of forty candles, and sang 'For they are jolly good fellows' for Marily and me, and 'Happy Birthday' for Laura.

Amanda and her children's last day had been a hot blue Sunday. We all swam and picnicked at Issos, and Marily took the younger ones into town for afternoon ice-creams, and we ate a final spaghetti supper all together in the open air. Peter sang 'Greensleeves' in his new chorister's voice. So ended a fortnight in which the six cousins had done nothing but simple things, and come to know each other – and their French opposite numbers – and to live together in friendship and harmony.

Katherine and hers stayed for two more weeks. The village filled up with visitors for the big holiday of 15 August. The season of weddings started. The open-air tavernas at the foot of our hill were packed every night, and the sounds of music and dancing floated over us till well into the small hours. On the 23rd the village kept its own Panayiri. The ikon of the Odhiyitria made her annual circuit of her territory, the bishop having come to join the usual cortège of attendants, followed by all her people, except the freethinkers in Spiro's café, who continued to play cards as she passed. Finally, the whole world congregated at the *plateia*. Spits turned, beer flowed, and

young and old linked hands in a giant wheel, spinning end-
lessly in the comradeship of the Corfu dance.

15

A Ramble round Aunt Muriel

Needing a break after the family invasion, we went to spend a weekend with Aunt Muriel. Muriel was not a real aunt of Marily's, but her father's only first cousin. However, being of the older generation, she preferred to be considered so.

We had seen her only a few times since our marriage. At that time she was the wife of a Cypriot doctor, George Spanopoulos, with whom she lived partly in Athens and partly in Cyprus. After his death, she made her principal home in Athens and only rarely came to Corfu, taking her summer holidays on a property she owned in Epirus, near the town of Preveza. She was elegantly undomesticated, fluent in several European tongues, immaculate in appearance, an avid and accomplished player of both bridge and Scrabble, and lived the life of an old-fashioned Athenian lady, in an old-fashioned Kolonaki apartment, with all her wants attended to by her devoted friend and servant Georgia.

Aunt Muriel was a British subject and indeed a baptised member of the Anglican Communion. She had been born Muriel Blakeney. A fair amount of history had gone into making her what she was.

The Blakeneys from whom she came were originally a Norfolk family. They had settled in Ireland in the reign of Queen Elizabeth I, and made their new home in Galway as members of the Anglo-Irish Ascendancy. In 1789, the year of the French Revolution, a son Robert was born who, at the age of fifteen, was commissioned as an ensign in the British Army. He served as an infantry officer in the Peninsula under Moore and Wellesley, and wrote an account of his experience there (later edited by one of his descendants, and published in 1899 by John Murray). He continued his military career after the final defeat of Napoleon, retiring with the rank of captain in 1828.

Before their occupation by the French revolutionary forces in 1797, the Eptanisa – the seven Ionian islands which lie off the coast of Greece from Albania to the Peloponnese – had been Venetian possessions for 400 years. The mainland, on the other hand, was in 1815 entirely Ottoman Turkish. The islands were by now held, *de facto*, by Great Britain. Faced with the problem of their future, the Great Powers of Europe came up with the solution of an independent state of the Ionian Islands, under a British Protectorate. The ordinary people of the islands, being Greeks, were naturally not consulted about these arrangements.

The British regarded this as no more than their due. They built a fine new palace in Corfu town and installed in it, as Lord High Commissioner, Sir Thomas Maitland, who treated the local senators with boorish contempt. They also set up what amounted to a colonial administration and maintained a strong naval and military presence. This was mainly concentrated on Corfu, which, as in Venetian times, and with its two fortresses, was the new state's capital and strategic base. The most vivid memorial to this miniature empire is the British Cemetery, on the outskirts of the town, still a shady and well-tended resting place for the many young men, and often their wives and children, for whom a posting to Corfu meant death from malaria, typhoid fever, or dysentery.

It seems probable that Robert Blakeney served as a soldier in the Ionian Islands. After taking his discharge he obtained official civilian appointments there, and was certainly a British consular agent before 1837. (The royal arms which he was entitled to display included, on an inescutcheon, the arms of the House of Hanover, a device discontinued by Queen Victoria on her accession.) More to the point, he showed good sense, and a good Irish heart, by falling in love with and marrying a beautiful Corfiot. Maria Balbi's family were Italian from Venice, but had settled in Corfu a generation before.

The marriage produced three daughters and one son. The girls all married Englishmen and left the Corfu stage. The boy, born in 1840 and christened Charles Altavilla, followed his father into the British consular service. By this time the political geography had considerably altered. The Greek War of Independence, begun in 1821, led to the recognition, in 1830, of the new sovereign state of Greece. Its northern land frontier ran from the Gulf of Volos, on the Aegean, to the large Ionian inlet of the Gulf of Arta, its southern shore becoming Greek, while the northern remained Turkish. This border remained virtually unchanged for the rest of the century. However, in 1864 Britain agreed to the cession of the Ionian Islands to the Greek kingdom.

Charles Altavilla Blakeney was British consul first in Albania, at the port of Santa Quaranta (the Forty Saints), which the Greeks know as Ayia Saranda, and the Albanians as Sarande. He then served at Missolonghi, and from 1874 till 1899 at Preveza, the port on the northern, Turkish, side of the narrow mouth of the Gulf of Arta. The town is now neither lively nor prosperous, but was then important as a frontier post of the Sultan's domain, and the port of entry for the regional capital at Arta. Several major trading nations maintained consulates there.

C.A. Blakeney not only represented his country at Preveza; he married the daughter of a leading citizen, Virginia Konemenou. The Konemeno family were, like most of the population of Epirus, Greeks and patriots. In 1716, when the Turks made their last attempt to take Corfu, they had fought for the Venetians and been rewarded by the grant of an estate on the shores of the gulf, near the village of Ay. Thoma (Preveza having fallen into Venetian hands in 1717). Virginia's father Nikolaos was clever and able. He worked for the Greek cause, and was considered something of a radical for writing in demotic Greek and encouraging its use as a literary language. Despite this background, he became for a time the Turkish consul in Corfu, and may have come to know the Blakeneys there. (A bust of Nikolaos Konemenos still stands in one of Preveza's public streets.)

Through his alliance with the family, Blakeney acquired the property known as Skafidaki, part of the Ay. Thoma estate, comprising about twenty-five acres and a thousand olive trees. There was a small dwelling hosue in the grove, habitable enough in spite of having no internal sanitation – a common feature of even quite grand country houses on Corfu well into the twentieth century. The Blakeneys later added a bathroom extension, along with a water closet. This last was the first ever seen in the district, and was a wonder to all.

Charles Altavilla and Virginia had one son, also named Charles, who was born in 1880, and three daughters. Besides their principal residence in Preveza, they owned Balbi property, including a town house, in Corfu. They also inherited, from some Polish connections, a house in Athens. The Foreign Office, which in those days showed a paternalist concern for the officers it appointed and controlled, paid for young Charles's education at an English boarding school. (This no doubt contributed to the impression which he always gave of a well-bred, good-humoured English gentleman.) In about 1902 – by which time his father had become consul in Corfu – he too joined the service, and was posted to the Serbian capital, Belgrade. He was still there when the 1914-18 war broke out. In 1915 an Austrian offensive drove the Serbian army back to the Adriatic coast. Charles was caught up in this retreat, and in the evacuation of many Serbs to Corfu, and was thus dramatically re-united with his family.

The Blakeney and Bulgari families became linked in the following year, when Charles married Lydia, daughter of Papa Constanti Bulgari, former priest of the church of St Spyridon, and sister of Papa Stephano, Marily's grandfather. Lydia was not the first, nor was she to be the last, Bulgari girl to marry an Anglos. (It is vain for a Welshman, Irishman or Scot to try to persuade Greeks that he is not English. Do not encyclopaedias, for use in Greek schools, contain an entry for Great Britain which reads: 'Another name for England'?) Papa Constanti had had a younger sister, Theodora, who married a Royal Navy chaplain, always known in the family as Pastor Goodrich. He came to visit the church, met the priest, at that time Theodora's uncle, and fell in love with the niece. (Their daughter, May, in her old age, was present at our wedding, as were Lydia and Uncle Charlie.)

Muriel was born in 1917, in the parsonage of the Anglican consular church in Corfu. Once the Great War was over, Charles returned to Serbia, now part of the new state of Jugoslavia, taking with him his wife and two-year-old daughter. He served as British consul in Belgrade, and later in Bucharest, and Muriel's girlhood was spent in these foreign capitals and among the cosmopolitan consular community. Naturally, she learned to speak good French and German, and some Serbo-Croat and Romanian, along with the English and Greek of her parents. Her English was faultless, though with an intonation telling of an upbringing outside England, and a characteristic burr, all her own, to the letter R. She was a tall, handsome girl, athletic and an excellent swimmer. Before the second war she was ranked the third best lady tennis player in Romania.

Summer leave was always spent at Skafidaki, for which she had a warm affection. The war brought the Blakeneys back to Athens, and it was there that Muriel was married, in a pink wedding dress.

We had a long-standing invitation to stay with her at her beloved Skafidaki, so we put the yellow Suzuki on board the ferry to Igounenitsa and headed south along the coast to Preveza. Some way short of the town one bumps into one of those outcrops of ancient history which turn up unexpectedly in Greece, and tend to divert the narrative into byways. On an eminence overlooking the road there was a jumble of fallen masonry, with some of the facings boldly inscribed in Latin. Looking over the plain below, we could trace the crumbled cincture of a city wall, enclosing an area large even by modern standards. It is the eloquent monument to a decisive moment in history.

Across the Preveza narrows juts Cape Actium, off which Octavian's fleet routed that of Mark Antony, sent him and Cleopatra scuttling to Egypt, and made Octavian, as Caesar Augustus, master of the Mediterranean world. He had pitched his tent, before the battle, on the height above the road. On the same spot he caused to be erected a vainglorious memorial in his own honour. He also ordered the building of a city, to be called Nikopolis, City of Victory. To people it, he uprooted and transported the population of several towns, the largest being Ambracia, ancient capital of King Pyrrhus, and the site of modern Arta. They were, after all, only Greeks. Today only the Greeks remain. The Romans have vanished, and the Bulgars sacked Nikopolis, leaving scarce one stone upon another.

So at last we arrived at Skafidaki, after many misdirections and false trails. A rough track wound to the old house and its little garden, hidden among the olives. Aunt Muriel had sloughed off her Athenian sophistication, and was living like a simple countrywoman – helped to do so, it must be said, by the care of the village family who oversaw the property in her absence, and brought her cooked meals by motor-cycle. Marily painted among the twisted olive trunks, and we swam in the shallow consommé of the Ambracian gulf. Across the water shimmered the orange groves of the Arta plain, and the long spit of Salaora, where the pelicans glide on the sea like swans. And in the evenings, instead of Scrabble, Aunt Muriel reminisced and unrolled her family history.

16

Autumn Leaves

Thursday, 31 August At 5 a.m. a distant trundling of grand pianos with flashes of lightning. Rain began at 6 with thunderclaps, and continued till 9. Then sunshine till noon, when the next lot of rain came in from the north-west. Marvellously welcome after the summer drought. Later, I assaulted an army of brambles, two levels down the hillside.

A real Greek supper – Irene's taramosalata; *kolokythia* stuffed with mince and rice, in egg and lemon sauce; *yiaourti*, figs and Isabella grapes from our own vine; all washed down with retsina.

Saw a fat brown snake in the garden, unidentified.

Friday, 1 September. M. and I picked flowers and lemons in the garden of the old house, which looks neglected and sad. In the evening at Lefteri's, before meeting Gerald and Margaret at the airport.

Sunday, 3 September Fiftieth anniversary of the outbreak of war – that too was a Sunday. Remembered that sunny morning at the house on the Spey in Rothiemurchus.

To lunch chez Mulder at Nisaki. Drove through rain, which cleared. A Panas family reunion – Mary and Fred, and her three brothers each with wife, meeting all together for the first time for thirty-seven years, they said. Six couples in all, and all having survived forty years of marriage.

Tuesday, 5 September Set off in rain for Kodhraka. Called at Mesonghi on the way, but the Count and Katie were out.

Dry down the coast. Gerald, Margaret and I swam from a quiet beach at Kodhraka, while M. painted. Then to old Karydi's place at Boukari for a drink and *meze* of *kalamarakia* (small squid).

In the afternoon George Manessi took Gerald to try windsurfing at Korissia, but they returned defeated by a Force 6 wind there, and huge waves on the other coast. George says that my fat snake was a European legless glass lizard. According to him the dinosaurean agama lizards in our garden are rare in Greece, found only on Corfu and two other islands. They are rumoured to have come here in the straw wrapping of the bottles of champagne, which the Kaiser used to drink, with oysters, when watching the sunset from Pelekas.

Thursday, 7 September Gerald and I left the house at 7.15 and climbed to Ayia Kyriaki. A lovely dawn, but the church very decrepit.

We all drove to Kalami, called on Andrea and Semira Kourousopoulo, and swam at the little bay below the White House, where the Durrell family lived pre-war. Now an indifferent restaurant. A poor meal, brightened by a pair of kingfishers over the water.

After supper, a final Scrabble match (won as usual by Margaret) before they set off for the mainland.

Friday, 8 September (Nativity of the Panayia) E.'s left on the ferry. M. and I then went to Kopanous chapel for the service, scheduled for 8.30. Found that it was now to start at ten, so came home and tried again later. Meanwhile Irene returned from town with fish from the market for a *kakavia* soup. She had been to see her doctor (more precisely, one of her many doctors). He was offered, and accepted, 2,000 drachmas to see her before normal consulting hours.

The little church looked well, carpeted with fresh bay leaves. Sergio and Maria were there with the two children, who took communion, along with a recently baptised infant and the very old man who lives opposite, now almost in his second childhood. Collected a lot of *artous* (blessed loaves) and took them to Mesonghi. Took coffee with the Count.

Katherine rang to say that all her children have Corfiot nits in their hair.

Monday, 11 September Elena Manessi flew to London to have her gallstones seen to. M. and I went to Ay. Yanni for a swim. George came sailing on his windsurfer from the other end of the beach, handsome and skilful. We all swam, in clear cool water.

We went to an evening performance of Euripides' *Bacchae* (the first Greek tragedy I read at school) at the municipal theatre. An intense, if eccentric, interpretation by the small Attis company from Thessaloniki, directed by Theodoros Terzopoulos. Six players, all on stage throughout. Highly stylised, almost balletic production, never dull. The text was a modern Greek translation, but some of the choruses were spoken in the classical original. Euripidean Greek is not too hard for today's audience, and the device both provided contrast and emphasised the continuity of Greek language and culture. Marina Kondou, our women's association president, was there with her husband.She wants to start amateur dramatics in the village. The cake of custom is starting to crumble.

The garden is full of pink lilies. Irene told Marily that they are the variety which grew at the foot of Christ's Cross, and that she had seen a photograph of this.

Picked the first fig from one of our young trees. A day of contentment.

Thursday, 12 September A blue tit – the first I have seen here this year – knocked itself out against one of the windows. After coming round it sat in a dazed way, turning its head from side to side. M. offered it a saucer of water in case it felt faint. I took its photograph. At the camera's click it immediately flew off.

M. left for Athens in the afternoon, to see her mother and Daisy. She took lemons, Isabella grapes, lilies and a large bunch of pink cyclamens, all from our garden, and a loaf of Hector's bread.

Wednesday, 13 September Fine hot weather continuing. Went to Kyr Yanko at Kouramades for a haircut, and then on to Ay. Gordi beach. Still very quiet at 10.30. Water like silk. Bought dark red plums, of the locality, and came back by Kato Garouna, below hillsides of olive and cypress, in slanting September light.

M. came on the evening plane, an hour and a half late. We bought a cooked chicken and chips at the Tsaros for our supper.

Thursday, 14 September Tou Stavrou (Holy Cross Day). We had thought of going into town, to hear the choir at the Saint, Irene having indicated firmly that it was our duty to go to church today. In the end we went down to our local, if only to hear she and Gerasimos sing the hymns of the Feast, less melodiously but with greater verve.

A full kirk, decorated with red ribbons and pink lilies. About forty children were massed at the front, imperfectly controlled by the schoolmaster. Irene sang the Creed. Most of our old friends were there – old Vasili and his Zaira, Leni, Spiro Mantou, etc. Mantou looks a bit low. His Olga has been in hospital again, and we suspect that the news is not good. We scooped him and Leni up and brought them home for coffee and *koniak*, to celebrate the day and cheer them up. Our Olga joined us and we had a village gossip on the terrace. Afterwards M. got Kimon to open the church again, so that she could do a sketch of it, and I take some photographs.

Gerald and Margaret got back from their trip. They had found the hotels indifferent, with awful breakfasts – well, this isn't Scotland – but everything O.K. otherwise. We doubt if they made much contact with people, what with the language problem and their natural reserve. A pity. People, finally, is what Greece is really about. For supper we ate a mousaka, which Irene had flavoured with sugar, instead of salt. Interesting.

Saturday, 16 September M.'s birthday. Olga and Irene full of good wishes. Olga presented a poem she had written, not hot on rhyme or spelling, but straight from the heart. The second verse can be roughly translated thus:

> My gift is small, but great my love,
> My heart's wish is that you should have
> Many sweet years, which like the spring
> May bless you with fresh blossoming.
>
>   With love and respect, Your friend Olga

She has been a most willing helper all summer, loves the children, and they her.

Jane Christodoulidis and her papa (Andrea Kourouso-poulos) came to lunch. Corfiot *bourdetto* fish stew, rich in red pepper, and other Greek trimmings, and a fair slosh of ouzo and wine. They are good company. Jane expects her first in February. Her Emilios was last year's prize law student at Edinburgh University and won the Faculty scholarship. He goes on now to his doctorate. Andrea says he has always been Top, in spite of his vague manner and hairy appearance.

All to Ileana's for evening drinks, and to meet the manager of Barclay's Corfu branch, and two chaps, one English and one Greek, from the British Council in Athens. Neither appeared distinguished. The Englishman, Taylor, is small and bearded, and was wearing, *mirabile visu*, a khaki bush jacket with trousers to match. I complimented him on his outfit, and he said it was part of the Raj. But his wife is nice. They are here for the start of the University of Corfu's academic year, why was not made clear. T. says he is keen to run a

Scottish Festival in Athens in 1991, with the Scottish National Orchestra and all the things which have made Scotland
great – haggis, bagpipes and much whisky. Hoots awa! But a
good party with lots of Greek friends.

Last night the moon, one day past the full, was almost
bright enough in the small hours to read by. At 7.30 this
morning it was setting like a huge pale sun.

Sunday, 17 September Spent most of the day at Lizzie's house
at Paleocastritsa, in part a duty visit to water her garden.
Weather still magnificent, and the sea delicious. (We have
had some matchless swimming this year.) Had her little
beach to ourselves, so M. cast off her bathing suit with
abandon and plunged in naked. Dead on cue a boat with
three German boys came round the point, and she had to
dodge behindthe rocks and get me to fetch her a pareo.

Ate our picnic at the house, with ouzo, and rested in one
of the bedrooms. After one or two false starts M. did a
water-colour of plants on the terrace. Watered, and came
away. When we left, the Ionian dazzled the eye with a
myriad sparks of sunlight – Aeschylus's countless laughter of
the waves.

Monday, 18 September Brother Stevie took us to a performance of *Aida* at the Municipal theatre. Like the *Bacchae*, part
of this year's official Festival. It was given by the Bulgarian
National Opera company of Varna, which are also present-
ing Carmen and Mozart's *Requiem*. The Mayor is strongly
PASOK, and keen on East Europeans. The town has even
sprouted posters in Bulgarian, doubly unintelligible because
of the Cyrillic script.

Corfu's answer to Luxor. An achievement to get it on to
our stage at all. Even without elephants, the chorus were
packed shoulder to shoulder. They sang well, and the dancing was graceful, but the soloists were no more than sound,
second-rank artists. The role of Aida was sung with feeling –

the girl had an enchanting pianissimo. Unhappily, she was six inches taller than Rhadames, even in his built-up shoes.

The opera started late and went on and on, with protracted intervals. The upstairs foyer, which I saw for the first time, contrasts sadly with the elegant and well-designed entrance and auditorium. It remains a barn-like space. No proper bar, just a long table and bottles coming out of ice-boxes below. At 12.30 a.m., with one act still to go, we left and went to Bekios's and consumed liver and a bottle of Elissar.

Thursday, 21 September Stepped outside in the early hours. Garden ghostly under a high last quarter moon. Orion was striding up the southern sky, the dog at his heels just clearing the treetops – my first sight of them this summer.

Dog and bird trouble today. Koula's Penelope is swooning about our property with a troop of suitors – found one of them on the terrace, with front paws on the parapet, admiring the view. A great tit flew into the hour during breakfast and kept on crashing into the windows. No sooner was it rescued than there was a thud outside the picture window, and we found a semi-conscious chiff-chaff on the sill. M. got it on its feet and fetched the studio saucer of water for it to drink while I took its picture. (Has the blue tit been spreading my fame around?)

The Vouli has voted (PASOK abstaining) to send Papandreou for trial on charges of corruption and telephone tapping. He treats the whole business with disdain, sends written statements denying everyting, and has not been near parliament since the election. Meanwhile, PASOK paint it all as a witch-hunt. Locally, green insults about Fascists and Traitors have re-erupted on the walls. The village mind is difficult to read. When M. suggests to people that the governmental scandals have sullied the fair name of Greece, and that dishonesty at the top seeps right down through society, their faces shut down, and silence falls.

The Ehrmans are back at Spartila. They had rung us from England to invite us to eat there tonight, having no telephone at the house. Their son Tom is there with them. He is a plant geneticist, reading for a Ph.D. Says that the aerial spray used here for the olive trees has been banned in Western Europe as carcinogenic. Assuming this to be so, one wonders a) how much one should worry, b) what on earth can one do about it. The information did not spoil an excellent evening, or the high-cholesterol dinner cooked by Aphrodite.

Friday, 22 September Leonidas called to discuss this winter's olive harvest, which promises well. We drank to its success, M. and I in *koniak*, he in peppermint liqueur, being the only thing in my cupboard he said his constitution would allow.

I slipped down to Ay. Yanni for a swim. M. spent most of the day cooking a special meal for what might I suppose be described as our dining circle. We squashed the whole dozen of us round the kitchen table, which made for a lively and deafening evening. (The Molyvadas reported that the Bulgarian *Carmen* was abysmal, and they left at half-time.)

Saturday, 23 September Heavy, damp day, but no rain. A good picking of green beans.

In the evening M. and I walked down to the Kamareli property which Spiro cultivates. He and his son Niko were repairing and improving an old barn. Behind the little house they have an untidy area inhabited by free-ranging hens, then a walnut and nespola grove leading to a pasture, and a fenced garden filled with various kinds of beans, cabbages, leeks, salads and some flowers. All very well kept. At the back tall old olives. The donkey was in its stable, in disgrace for having kicked the goat, to its fatal injury. Spiro was upset, and said it was his own fault for misjudging the tethering distance. We picked, broke and ate fresh walnuts, and discussed rural affairs. Spiro has an exact knowledge of all the families of our district and their many peculiarities, and of how land ownership has

changed from one generation to another. Later that night
Nina and he brought us eggs and a large bag of walnuts.

Out of idleness we ate at Lefteri's. Spiro the Father-in-Law
was there, drinking beer with Maki the tree-cutter. He wanted
to stand us our retsina, so we paid for their beer. This recipro-
cal generosity added to the stock of mutual good will and
cost nothing except the difference in price between the two
drinks – slightly in their favour. We arranged for him to come
tomorrow to discuss autumn work.

Sunday, 24 September Saw the first robin. They winter here,
but are all gone by the time we arrive in spring. I don't know
to which part of Europe they go to breed. Their song en-
hances our woodland music, and they come about the house,
much bolder than the permanent residents, mostly blackcaps
and Sardinian warblers. Today's bird sat on the terrace parapet
and fixed me with a speculative eye.

M. started a painting of the interior of the church, based on
her sketch and my photos the other day.

Cecil came to collect a tape he had lent us, of a conversation
with his friend Colin Semper, Canon of Westminster – to
be broadcast on Radio Four, he says. The old man's liveliness of mind is extraordinary. He attributes it, in part, to his
adherence to the teaching of Gurdjieff. Nor are his physical
faculties much impaired. He still pilots his car as if it were one
of his first World War aeroplanes. This can be alarming. The
last time that the four of us went out to dinner, he insisted on
driving, and en route bounced off two walls and a parked
motor-car, each time proceeding on his way with a careless
laugh.

While he was with us, the Father-in-Law appeared, to put
off this evening's meeting. When Cecil learned that he was the
village gravedigger he said that he would be needing his services any day now, and asked the price of a new grave. Spiro
said 20,000 but for someone known to him only 15,000, which
Cecil thought very reasonable. He went on to give an account

of a funeral at which he had been waiting in the grave for the corpse to arrive. The Thin One (sc. Kosta the fat butcher) nudged a small mourner so that he fell into the grave, and he, Spiro, began to shovel earth over him. After a profitable discussion about our olive trees, he left inviting us to come and eat *giouvetsi* with him and family.

Eventually got away to drive to St George of the Ices, where we found a crowd of friends and had a jolly swim and picnic. The top of the beach was full of white sand lilies. Ileana dug up two for us – a labour of love, for the bulbs were at least half a metre deep.

On the way home took an ouzo off the Ricketts, just here after four days hard driving across Europe. The house, a converted *litrouvio*, so calm and welcoming in the big grove.

Monday, 25 September Cousin Dale and his Hermione arrived at lunchtime, having left home in Gifford at 4 a.m. They brought the news that Jim Kilbrandon died a couple of weeks ago. Unusual, accomplished man. An adornment of the law in Scotland, yet he sat lightly to his profession – one remembers him rather as a good man.

Tuesday, 26 September Took D. and H. to call on the Count in town. He was in good spirits. His book, an account of old Corfiot town houses and the families who owned them, is at the printer. He says he is thinking of writing a family history – he has his whole genealogy in his head and once dictated it to me without a single hesitation. Only, he is eighty-four, and doesn't have a word processor like Cecil. We doubt if the work will come to fruition.

Thence to Spartilas, where we found John, Susan and Tom back from a trip to Zagoria and the Pindus foothills. Susan and Tom had walked from Papingo over to Skommeli, below Mount Tymphi. They hope to start their *trygo* (vintage) tomorrow. Aphrodite gave us a huge bunch from the pergola. We went on up through the village, and found a picnic spot on a rocky bluff with two fine old stone threshing floors. Olives below the road, and above pale rocks and aromatic garigue. M. found a colchicum cupanii in flower.

While we were waiting to go out with Cecil and Fanny for supper, Tryphon dropped in on his way from golf with a boring insurance man called Cholmley, pronounced Chumly, Lewis from Surrey. They took a drink and departed, and the rest of us went to the Gloupos taverna down the road. Some elegant and athletic Greek dancing, but so noisy that no conversation was possible. The three men at the table had all been in Athens on Christmas Day 1944 – Cecil RAF, Dale RN, I RA.

Thursday, 28 September Early drizzle turned to torrents, with thunder and lightning. A bootless morning. At noon a clearance allowed us to go to town, for sightseeing and lunch. In our absence the Father-in-Law left wine and walnuts on our doorstep.

Suddenly, so cool in the evening that we lit a fire for the first time since spring.

Friday, 29 September Yesterday's rain has almost filled our cistern. Picked a big crop of eans.

The Ricketts came to lunch, bringing Desmond Shawe Taylor, the music critic. Elizabeth also came over from Liapades. Irene had cooked her special chicken, flavoured with garlic, pepper, lemon and oregano, and grilled slowly over charcoal for three hours – with roast potatoes and the new beans, as fine a dish as ever chef conceived. Stewed quinces with a cream and *yiaourti* whip to follow. It grew darker and darker during the meal, culminating in a grand black thunderstorm. Rain so intense that we had to ferry the guests to their cars in our own.

In the evening, we included D. and H. in our invitation to drinks in HMS *Coventry*, docked at the New Port. She is the sixth of her name, newly commissioned to replace the one lost in the Falklands war. Technically a frigate, she is, at 5,000 tons, about as large as an old second-class cruiser, with a complement of 250. She is powered by two aircraft-type engines, and can accelerate from stationary to thirty knots in seventy-five seconds.

On account of the rain, the party had been transferred from the deck to the helicopter hangar. Impressive and charming captain, Ted Hackett, and nice hospitable officers. Dale was delighted at being on board a Royal Navy ship again and had a long talk with the surgeon commander. There were the usual lot of official guests – Pippa our consul, and two former consuls, John Forte and Pat Karydi; the R.C. Bishop, and Father Tsitsa from the Saint, representing the Orthodox, chatting ecumenically; Rev. Bond, the Anglican chaplain, alone and looking as miserable as ever, not much of an advertisement for the Faith; assorted Anglo-Hellenic veterans like ourselves. Colours were lowered, with bugles, at nine o'clock.

Come to think of it, I have never before been in a British warship. M.'s last visit was to Mountbatten's flagship of the Mediterranean Fleet in 1949, shortly before we were married.

Saturday, 30 September Neither of us slept well. In my case three large brandies may have contributed, in M.'s a draught of neat gin from a tumbler given her by a rating in mistake for water. Thunder rumbled all night like a distant artillery barrage. By morning all sparkling.

Olga came very upset, having learned that one of her sons-in-law has an inoperable brain tumour. They have two children and have worked hard to establish a successful small restaurant at Barbati.

Dale and Hermione took us out to Gouveli's fish restaurant at Mandouki. He was a fisherman and tells splendid tales of voyages all over the eastern Mediterranean. Now he pads round bare-footed serving the tables. His wife cooks fish soup and fish and sea-food of various kinds, all fresh, nothing else – if you want afters, you go on elsewhere. We ate well, with wine, for six pounds a head. A dozen officers from Coventry arrived and made a big table outside, with Captain Ted in their midst. (Dale says such democracy was unheard of in his RN days.) Ices and coffee at the town *plateia*.

Sunday, 1 October Very damp day with heavy rain on and off. I went to the Pahatika church. Papa Thanasi standing in, brisk as ever. Old Gerasimos was in overpowering voice, and Irene sang the Trisagion with elaborate grace notes (*kourones* or crowns, she calls them).

Old Olga called. She has to go to Ioannina tomorrow with her 'rosebud'. The old wretch insists on seeing an eye-doctor there. Says he can't find glasses which are any good – no wonder, after a lifetime of alcohol and nicotine. He also has a set of false teeth which are too uncomfortable to wear. Olga wonders if they could be sold. 'They've hardly been worn at all,' she says. One owner, low mileage.

17

Bands, Barcaroles and Baroque

Bombs and *bouzouki* between them all but banished, for ever, the Italian sweetness which used to distinguish Corfiot music from that of mainland and Aegean Greece. Many years ago – when I first knew the island – one might be startled by a roar of polyphonic Verdi, erupting from the depths of a workmen's wineship. Four-part harmony, as of a barber shop quartet, would lure one round a corner to where a hired serenade floated from the shadows to a lady's balcony. Or, at a dim table of an old-fashioned taverna, a lone singer would soliloquise to his guitar in a plaintive Venetian cantada.

These voices are long silent. The role of the wartime bombing was to damage beyond repair the town's elegant small opera house. Here Neapolitan and Apulian touring companies had for generations made the arias of *Rigoletto, La Traviata* and *The Barber* common coin of the Corfiot musical currency. Now the source was dry. Perhaps it would have happened without bombs. Mussolini's military occupation brought disenchantment with all things Italian, and encouraged the islanders to assert their Greekness, rather than Ionian peculiarity.

Meanwhile, the *bouzouki*, most un-Ionian of instruments, was biding its time. As late as 1960 it was mostly to be heard in its own special Athenian shrines. These were garishly lit platforms, scattered between the city and the sea-front at Phaleron, on which bands of eight or ten *bouzoukia* accompanied powerful ladies in long white dresses, with lungs to match their bosoms, in ear-splitting ditties of Athenian low life. Then, two or three musicians of genius captured and

tamed this wild steed of the Romaic ethos, and harnessed it
to the chariot of their melodic inspiration. Film, disc and
transistor did the rest. Within a couple of years Hadzidakis
and Thodorakis had made the Greek popular song, and the
seductive insistence of the *bouzouki*, known everywhere in
the West. They invaded every bar and taverna in Corfu, and
spilled out into the streets by day and night.

The old music least affected by this revolution was that
created by the island bands. These nurses of indigenous talent
and civic pride became established, at least in their present
form, during the nineteenth century. The two senior, and
most sophisticated were, and are, those of the capital. The
Philarmoniki and the Mantzaro (named after the Corfiot
composer who set to music Solomos's Hymn to Liberty,
making it Greece's national anthem) both have their headquarters in the heart of the old town. Elegantly painted
signboards, and the random discords of practising tubas and
trombones, advertise the upper chambers where they re-
hearse.

Soon some of the larger villages set up in emulation. The
fashion spread until there were a dozen or so wind ensembles
scattered over the island. Our own village Philharmonic –
officially the Omonia, or Concord, but familiarly known as
the Music (i Mousiki) – has its year of foundation stated on
the front of the Syllogo as 1896. Rivalry between villages
was a spur to the quality of both performance and appearance. Boys – and in recent years girls – were encouraged to
learn an instrument from an early age, often starting in flute
or clarinet and graduating to trumpet and the heavier brass.
Others would begin on the kettle-drum and work up to the
side or the big drum. As a result, almost every man in the
village was competent on one instrument or another. Spiro
the Father-in-Law still blew a useful trombone, and bald
Niko could be called on to do a vigorous act on the big
drum.

All players, of whatever age of size, wear the uniform.

The standard colour is dark blue. Some bands, like ours, also assume a lightweight white in summer. Each village has its own distinctive coloured piping. The crowning splendour is the helmet, of brass or silver, with its horse-hair plume of colours to match the edging of the jacket. With helmets polished as brilliantly as the trumpets, tubas and trombones, a Corfu band has a swagger to lift the hearts of its supporters as nobly as any football team.

The original purpose of these musics was, and still principally is, to accompany and dignify the various Litanies of the Orthodox religion.

These processions, in which the relic or ikon of a saint is carried from its permanent home in church, either to another chapel or shrine, or on a circular tour of its district, take place usually on the saint's own feast day, or that of the chapel to be visited. There is also the Good Friday Litania, observed by every working church, of the Epitaphion, or funeral bier of Christ. For all of these the bands provide solemn music, to supplement the singing of priest and choir.

Corfu is special in holding four Litanies each year in the town, commemorating public miracles of its patron saint, Spyridon. The preserved body of the thaumaturge is taken from his massive silver casket, set standing upright in a light travelling receptacle (with his head visible through a small window), and borne ceremonially round the Plateia and part of the town. The saint is preceded by groups of cassocked acolytes with crosses, banners and lanterns and by numerous contingents of pupils from the boys' and girls' high schools, of boy scouts and girl guides, and from the armed forces. Finally, the bishop, following two files of priests in canonicals bright as a flower garden, walks directly in front of the canopied casket from which radiate blessing and healing to believers.

Spaced out along the length of the procession are not only the town bands (now three, an acrimonious disruption having spawned a New Philarmoniki, all in scarlet) but several from the villages. They generally contrive by playing in succession, to provide continuous and varied background music. Faulty communications, however, can lead to simultaneous competition between two consorts, causing hideous discords, and disarray among the schoolchildren trying to slow march in time with the music.

This having been in the past practically the sole function of the bands, particularly in the villages, it was not surprising that their repertoire was limited. It consisted, in the main, of slow marches and a few, even slower, pieces of reverential solemnity, deemed suitable for addressing an iconic Virgin. The town bands rehearsed a wider selection for recitals given on summer evenings from the ornate Victorian bandstand on the upper Esplanade, but these rarely ventured beyond the familiar homeground of Puccini and Sousa. Only in the year of which I have been writing did I sense the signs of breakthrough. Within a month I heard, first, the Old Philarmoniki practising 'Auld Lang Syne', and later the Mantzaro in full cry after Ravel's Bolero.

Tradition keeps another, less flamboyant, champion in the Corfu Municipal Choir. This has won enough international reputation to take part in choral events as far away as Wales. Our personal consciousness of it came about through our friendship with Costaki Botsi, whose wife Inez was an active contralto member. At the time of Daisy's visit in July they invited Marily and me to be their guests at the choir's Barcarola. This is a Corfiot magnification of the lay of the gondolier, into a water-borne performance by the entire choir, with invited artists. It is in keeping with the island penchant for the picturesque – moonlit gardens fragrant with jasmine, or Venetian battlements among the wheeling constellations – as the setting for musical entertainment. We accepted of course, though with anticipation blunted by the news that our gondola was to be the car-ferry MV *Kerkyra*, and that 800 invitations had gone out.

Estimated time of departure was 2130, from the quay of the Watersport Club below the Old Fortress. The *Kerkyra* hove in sight round Caposidero at 2115, and we embarked and took our hard-bottomed seats on the car deck, facing the ramp at the bow, below which was the stage. At 2200 – briskly punctual for Corfu – we set off, to an announcement that the performance would last for three and a half hours, including an interval for refreshments. The mayor, inevitably, said a few words. The vessel sailed for about twenty minutes to a point in the gulf, off Benitses, where it stopped its engines. From the auditorium no part of the sea or land was visible because of the high sides of the deck. The concert then began.

The first part consisted of a series of Greek songs, all dating from before, some from much before, 1940. Most had verses sung solo by a member of the choir (the best was a girl from one of the few Hebrew families of Corfu to survive the wartime Nazi deportation), and a chorus by the whole body of about forty ladies and fifteen men. They were accompanied by a local lady on a vintage upright piano, and conducted by a strenuous Athenian lady in draperies. The selection of songs lacked variety, and the same could be said of their rendering. This was vigorous and tuneful, but spoiled by a constant sameness of style and arrangement.

The interval followed. Everyone was issued with a pre-packed snack of one small cheese pie, one very small meat ball, and a tub of chocolate mousse. Crisps and biscuits were also on sale at the ship's bar. Behind the seating on the deck a van had been parked, carrying a barrel of wine, served free in plastic cups to whoever wanted. About this time, a gibbous moon rose, very prettily, above the mountains of Epiros. Later, when it was overhead, we went to an upper deck in its milky light. The gulf was very still, reflecting the lights of Benitses and the lamps of *gri-gri* fishing boats far to the south. A lone fisherman rowed close from the darkness and stayed to listen to the music for a few minutes. It was cold enough for two jerseys, and we soon went below.

After the interval there was an instrumental interlude, given by the local *mandinolado* (mandoline orchestra). This comprised, along with its eight mandolines, two flutes and two clarinets, plus three guitars, which contributed a rhythmic bass. The leading mandolinists were two severely impassive middle-aged ladies. They presented a programme of popular music in absolutely strict tempo, with virtually no light and shade of tone or volume.

Part III restored the audience to life. The choir were joined by two professionals, a tenor from Athens and a baritone who was a native of Sophia's village, Chlomos. Most of the music was Italian and operatic and included a rendering by the tenor, complete with Carusoid sobs, of 'O Sole Mio', first in Italian and then in English. The Corfiot baritone accompanied himself on the Spanish guitar and was received with rapture. The climax was an unskilful arrangement for choir and solo bass voice, of 'Ol' Man River' sung in Greek by an elderly Corfiot whose party piece it had clearly been for many years, and who managed to finish nearly a semitone lower than the choir.

The organisation of the evening was good, the amplification system, by a variety of microphones and loudspeakers, less so. The electrician had problems in controlling his equipment, which emitted spasmodic squeals and detonations. The official photographer was, also, so obtrusive as to constitute an integral part of the concert. He was a young man with abundant hair and enormous nose and moustache. Clad in a red T-shirt, and with a bright green pullover slung about his neck, exiguous white shorts and trainers, he sprang manically around throughout the performance, taking pictures from every angle.

It was all amateur, in the true sense, and wholly *laiko*, of the people. The material was good, but its under-development betrayed, perhaps, the lack of the Western musical tradition. The performers had little to measure themselves against, and insufficiently critical hearers. But it felt more like the real Corfu Experience than any artificial village with pretend workshops and imported craftsmen, a homely family affair, without affectation. The audience was made up of decent working folk and their well-behaved children. We recognised nobody, and the *benestanti* (nobs) were conspicuously absent.

During the return voyage old Lia Aspioti's dance troupe, in costume, went through their routine of folk dances, and to end it all the choir and many of the audience joined in the familiar Corfu round dance on the deck, and *kefi* overcame respectability. We docked at 0220, and got home at 3 a.m., exhausted and ravenous, but glad to have been there.

The same moon, a week younger, had had a walking-on part in a piece of urban theatre. As an item in the so-called Corfu Festival, which saunters erratically through the summer months, the Youth Orchestra of the Rhineland-Palatinate, based at Mainz, gave a concert under the direction of the Greek conductor, Dimitri Agraphiotis. The two principal pieces were Beethoven's Third Piano Concerto and Dvorak's Eighth Symphony. The soloist was Agraphiotis's nineteen-year-old son, who had composed his own cadenza. He was a good-looking boy with a short Mozartean pony-tail, and the freshness and delicacy of the playing, of both pianist and orchestra, gave the concerto a feel of Wolfgang Amadeus rather than of Ludwig van. The Dvorak was exactly matched to the young players' capabilities, and was performed with both profundity and enthusiasm.

The sauce to the meal was the setting. The stage was erected in front of the south face of the seventeenth-century Venetian theatre which now houses the Demarcheion (Town Hall). The seats were ranged on the wide steps leading up to the big square. So we were looking at a façade of five arches, each surmounted by a large carved stone mask, and above a line of medallions with sculpted heads in profile and classical scenes, all thrown into relief by lighting from below. To the right, the west front of the Roman Catholic cathedral, of the same period, austerely elegant, with a square tower at the corner, was lit by a floodlight. To the left was a tall terrace of

Venetian-style flatted tenements, their plain frontage broken only by windows with wooden shutters and wrought-iron balconies.

Daylight faded as the music began, till the lighting dominated the square. Families looked down from the balconies, or strolled up and down the street in front of the cathedral. Odd couples and groups joined, or left, the audience as they pleased. A canary in a high cage trilled an obbligato, while Alpine swifts, disturbed from their roosts, dashed screaming above our heads. Three or four times a climbing aircraft almost drowned the orchestra. And the silver moon sailed up the sky behind us. A stage-set, in its way as Corfiot as the night on the *Kerkyra*.

Later that summer a notice appeared at Hector the baker's and other shops, of a concert to be given in the village school by a *sestetto pnefston* (wind sextet). This had been organised by the president of our local Women's Guild, Marina Kondou, but the moving spirit, and leader of the sextet, was her son Spiro, a clarinettist. The rest of the group (another clarinet, two flutes, a horn and a bassoon) were all young people from the district, including old Vasili's granddaughter Zaira, and a granddaughter of Spiro Mantou.

We were in our seats in the school classroom by 8.30 on the Sunday evening. There was a full attendance of supporters, headed by Taki the President, Papa Spiro and his sacristan, Kimon, the schoolmaster, and, of course, the two proud grandfathers. The room and everybody in it became extremely hot – Vasili explained that it had been decided not to hold the concert in the open air because of traffic and aircraft noise. The walls had their weekday decoration – a map of Greece, a chart of the seasons, and a picture of Jesus with some children. The blackboard had been neatly adorned with musical symbols, and with two 'urgent' messages:

1 Chamber music is not suited to children under six.
2 Please, no smoking.

The group gave a very creditable performance of a dozen short works, for various combinations of instruments, by composers from J.S. Bach and Telemann, through Handel and Mozart, to lesser known nineteenth-century figures. Young Spiro Kondos, the leader, had made his own arrangement of the six-instrument pieces. The star was Zaira, both on her flute, and in a guitar solo. For most of the village it was a rare – maybe unique – excursion into the realm of classical music.

18

A Sort of Spring

The late September rains transform Kapoutsi. In the hot months the tender flowers, the herbs and the tomatoes, peppers and aubergines, have been kept alive by constant watering. The tougher plants, roses and lavender, shrubs and trees, survive with little irrigation, but only by aestivating, conserving energy, as if holding their breath, till easier times return. On the open ground, the grass and small wild flowers die down and dry up, so that the terraces and slopes become a uniform brown. Everywhere leaves droop, dusty and listless.

A couple of nights of rain, preferably with one of the special thunderstorms which help to give us an annual rainfall equal to Glasgow's, are enough to re-start nature's circulation. The whole property, its face washed and shining, stretches its arms and pricks its ears. Within two or three days the brown earth is covered with a green fuzz, faint at first, then thickening to a new burgeon of grass and weeds.

Our autumn is more like a second spring than the season which induces romantic melancholy in poets of the north. There is almost no turn or fall of the leaf, no silent rain of yellow and brown to lay a dank carpet for the feet. On the olive trees any change of colour is in the fruit, which, as the rain swells them, turn from yellow-green to purple-brown, before deepening to jet. Under the trees the flowers appear.

The autumn is at once more startling, and more discreet, than the true spring. It startles because it is like a desert bursting into life; the real spring only moves from green to greener. On the other hand, nothing can rival the vitality of April and May. To those accustomed to the reluctant

daffodils and May Day snow flurries of Scotland, the efflores-
cence unrolls as breathlessly as a speeded-up film, from the
first anemones and dwarf mauve irises, through pale asphodel
and yellow of broom and corn marigold, to the explosion of
energy which whips the wistaria and white wild roses into
mad spirals round the dark spears of the cypresses.

In September the lilies of the Cross have been the forerun-
ners. Now they are echoed by clumps of leafless autumn
crocuses, whose slender white stalks give them the name of
'naked boys'. These in turn are shouted down by bold orange
sternbergias, made to look almost vulgar by smaller creamy
crocuses, and the frail narcissus serotinus, which has no trumpet to blow. Finally, all yield to myriads of *kopelloules* (little
maidens), the delicate Corfu cyclamens, strewing drifts of
pink over the woodland slopes and banks of the island.

Each of the two seasons has its special smell. In spring
the olive presses are still at their work of extracting the oil
which remains Corfu's principal product, and the proximity
of the process can be detected by a distinctive sour odour –
rather as breweries used to advertise their presence from afar.
The autumn scent is that of the vintage. Not many vines are
grown in our part of the island. However, any villager worth
his salt likes to make his own wine and buys grapes from
the lorries which come up from Lefkimmi in the south, or
from the islands of Cephallonia and Zante. These are pressed
in household tubs, vats or barrels, and for days on end the
fragrance of the juice floats through the lanes and stairs of
the village. The work is for male feet only, in contrast to
sweeping, a task popularly supposed to inhibit the growth of
one's moustaches. The wine is drunk very young, though not
before St Demetrios's Day on 26 October. A bottle is often
taken as a gift on visiting, and always commended as pure
and free from chemicals, though the quality varies from in-
triguing to valuable for vinegar.

Our autumn has one sharp scent common to autumns
everywhere. It is the season for bonfires. These are prohibited

during the dry months, and nobody who has seen the wreckage of an olive grove devastated by fire (it gets into the hollow bases of the trunks and blasts them apart) is likely to burn rubbish near his trees when all vegetation is flammable. Now, in October, the valleys are filled with drifting plumes of smoke, and my journal with almost daily entries of the burning of the summer's pruning, slashing and howking.

The only blemish on autumn is the shooting of small birds. The season begins in September with the ritual massacre of turtle doves, on the morning when the migrating flocks wing in from the Ionian. They are welcomed by a fusillade from the ridges, and end their journey with a trip into town dangling in sad rows from the handlebars of motor bikes. From then on, every dawn is greeted with the popping of shotguns in the olive groves. In Greece, as in Italy and the south of France, it is a matter of principle and prestige for a young man to own a gun and go hunting. The fact that there is nothing bigger than a blackbird in the woods is of no consequence – the rule is simple; if it flies, shoot it. Men even equip themselves with full camouflage uniforms, with peaked caps, the better to bag warblers.

Irene once told us that it used to be the custom - a relic of feudalism perhaps – to present a robin pie to the mistress of the big house on Christmas Day.

19

Patmos

In 1087, the year when William the Norman fell from his horse and left vacant the throne which he had won by conquest, the imperial throne at Constantinople was occupied by another capable ruler. The Empire needed one. When Alexios Comnenos became emperor of Byzantium in 1081, the Seljuk Turks, following up their victory at Manzikert ten years before, had swept across Asia Minor to reach the Sea of Marmara. Anatolia was lost, for ever, to the Greeks, and the capital city itself was under threat.

Meanwhile the restless Normans had driven the Greeks from southern Italy and established a kingdom in Apulia and Calabria. In the year of Alexios's accession their leader, Robert Guiscard, sailed his fleet across the Adriatic to capture Durazzo, the strongly fortified port from which the ancient Roman highway, the Via Egnatia, ran across the Balkans to Constantine's City.

Alexios needed all his courage and skill to counter these menaces from east and west, which he did with remarkable success. At the same time, as supreme and absolute ruler, in matters both temporal and spiritual, he was obliged to concern himself with all the domestic problems of his empire, whether civil or ecclesiastical. Of the latter, a new one emerged in 1087, in the person of the monk Christodoulos.

He was a holy man with a vision. During his years as a hermit in Asia Minor and on Cos – and possibly as an abbot – he had conceived the desire to found a monastery in honour of St John the Divine, the first Christian theologian, who had tried to fathom and, in his gospel and letters, to explain the nature and meaning of God, as shown forth in the person of Jesus of Nazareth. It was an integral part of the vision that the monastery should be established on the island of Patmos. Tradition was firm that John, exiled there by the Roman authorities, had experienced, in his old age, a divine revealing – an apocalypse - of the end of all things, and of a new heaven and a new earth. There was even a shrine, built round the cave – scarcely more than a rock cleft – where the evangelist was said to have heard the words of revelation, and dictated them to his disciple Prochoros.

Tradition was embroidered, not to its benefit, with tales of a conflict between John and an evil magician named Xynops, which ended with the latter being turned, in an un-Christian spirit, into stone. But whatever John may have done on Patmos, the island soil had indubitably been trodden by the feet of the Master's best friend, into whose care he had, at his death, entrusted his mother. It was, therefore, a Holy Place. What a consummation it would be, Christodoulos thought, if the whole island of Patmos could be monastic land, contributing to the material support of his foundation, and benefiting from its spiritual oversight and care.

Only the emperor had the power to make the dream come true. Christodoulos went to Constantinople, and sought an audience of the emperor. What argument swayed Alexios's heart, or what credit he thought he would win, cannot be known; but he directed the imperial scribes to prepare a conveyance to Christodoulos of the whole island of Patmos for the purpose he put forward, and when the long parchment scroll had been written he signed it in imperial vermilion. The year was 1087.

He knew where to build. The cave of the Apocalypse lay half way up the steep flank of the hill behind the island's little harbour. Above it the hill sharpened to a cone, with a summit platform, from which one could survey the southern half of the island, and keep a watch for pirates and enemy fleets. There Christodoulos and his followers laid the foundations for their little *katholikon*, the monastery church. Behind it, round a courtyard, grew up the essential buildings of a religious community – a refectory with its long stone table, equipped at each monk's place with a cubbyhole for his eating utensils, the kitchen with its massive store rooms and cellars, a library and scriptorium, the abbot's quarters and reception room for visitors, and the monks' individual cells.

From its inception the foundation flourished. Christodoulos died and was laid to rest in his separate chapel. Beatified, his relic became a goal for pilgrims. The monastery was much enlarged and, eventually, fortified with castellated walls, so that it came to resemble what in fact it was, a stronghold of the Orthodox faith. It also grew rich, and at one time maintained a small merchant fleet. So high was its prestige that the Ottoman sultans respected its independence.

During the seventeenth and eighteenth centuries a town, containing many affluent merchants' houses, grew round the monastery until it encircled the hilltop like a white wreath. At the same time, the serious spiritual influence of the monks encouraged the building, all over Patmos, of a number of churches, monasteries and convents out of all proportion to the island's mere thirty square miles. The old Patiniot families have now vanished from their houses in the town on the hill, leaving the courtyards and spacious rooms, behind the secretive whitewashed walls of the lanes, to be acquired as summer retreats by members of a wealthy international coterie with aesthetic leanings. But old-fashioned theology and devotion continue to thrive throughout the island, as Blessed Christodoulos intended that they should.

We went to Patmos for the Pentecost holiday weekend. (This was after we had lost Ina and Daisy.) Our Athenian friend Alexandra lent us the house, just outside the upper town, which she and her husband had created from two old cottages, with a central hibiscus-bright courtyard, and a view of fields yellow to harvest, picked out with dry stone walls and small white buildings marked out as churches by a dome, or barrel-vaulted roof and a vestigial apse.

George and Elena came with us. Together we explored the little island, swam from its beaches, and ate its lobsters. We also, of course, visited the Apocalypse chapel, now gravely tended by brothers from the small monastery of which it forms part. At the big monastery on the hilltop we saw, along with the illuminated manuscripts, gospel and service books, and the gold-embroidered vestments of the treasury, its unique pride, the emperor's deed of donation to Christodoulos.

After Sunday service, we went in search of Sister Efpraxia – Sister Good-Conduct one might call her, in the Bunyan idiom. Alexandra had asked us to give greetings to her at her convent, not far from the house. She was not difficult to find, there being only four nuns in the sisterhood. She was a small woman, probably around seventy, with a merry eye and un-lined face, like an almost ripe apricot. She immediately conducted us on a tour of the premises, skipping ahead of us, round corners and up staircases, but always announcing her whereabouts by trilling spiritual songs in a high girl's voice.

At last we came to rest outside her cell. She sat us down, made coffee, and as we drank regaled us with her life story and convent gossip. She had been one of a peasant family of twelve, dedicated to the religious life as a girl, and had never been outside the island, seldom indeed far from the convent gate. As she rattled on with innocent liveliness, she realised that I was not following much of her rapid-fire Patiniot Greek. She gave me a pitying pat on the knee and said kindly, 'He's illiterate [agrammatos], poor fellow'.

Sister Efpraxia then told us the true story of Blessed Christodoulos's visit to the emperor Alexios. At his first audience he made no impression and left empty-handed. On the next day the empress was taking heliotherapy (sunbathing) on her palace balcony when she saw a bearded figure, in monastic habit, floating past her in the air. She went down and found her husband. 'Alexi,' she said, 'who was the churchman you gave an audience to yesterday?' 'Some old monk,' replied the emperor, 'wanting an island off me.' 'Not just any old monk,' the empress said. 'He's a saint. He flies.' So they recalled Christodoulos, and hagiography merged into history.

That afternoon I took my camera for an outing up a track into open country beyond the town. At the top of a rise I came to a level place from which the land fell steeply to the sea far below. Here there was a low house, and hard by a little church, white against a clump of pink oleanders. A man and woman were clearing weeds, and two boys, of about ten and eight, wearing shorts and blue baseball caps, were sweeping the surrounds of the church. The older boy followed me inside, and introduced me to the various saints in the ikons on the walls. He told me that, as I had suspected, they were adorning the precinct for its *yiorti* on the morrow, the Feast of the Holy Spirit. But, he explained, priests were so much in demand that weekend that it would only be possible to sing Vespers on the day, with the Liturgy on Tuesday morning. I took a picture of him at the door, and then, at his insistence, another including his small brother as well.

On Tuesday morning I rose, virtuously, before sun-up. Even so, the service had almost ended by the time I reached the church. There was a congregation of about a dozen (including, I discovered, two Englishwomen). The psaltis was a tall thin young monk, very black and wild of hair and beard, like an aspiring John Baptist. My young friend, in a faded blue cassock, doubled as acolyte and thurifer. Most of the people took the sacrament. Then we were blessed and went out into the early sunlight, and ate sanctified bread and drank sweet coffee from plastic cups, between the white chapel and the dark Aegean, beckoning rhythmically to the west.

20

Peacocks and Paladins of Pelops

Before the black winter, we had planned with our London friends Patrick and Mary to make an expedition into the Peloponnese. We already knew Mycenae, Nauplion and Epidauros. This time our goal was the Deep Mani, the bony finger which Mount Taygetos points towards Africa. Its tip, Cape Tainaron (better known in the west as Matapan), is the very end of Greece and the legendary gateway to Tartarus. The Maniots were for centuries reputed for intransigence, guns and blood-feuds, and believe themselves, not without reason, to be the true descendants of the ancient Spartans. We all four felt it time to visit those remote and unspoiled parts, as an antidote to Corfu lushness, and we chose early summer as affording the best opportunity for finding flowers, and for Marily to paint.

The chosen driving route was from Patras down the west coast of the Peloponnese, by way of Olympia, to Pylos and Methoni, and thence through Kalamata to our destination, with a return journey, via Monemvasia and Sparta, through the heart of Arcadia to Kalavryta and the Gulf of Corinth. Thus we would zig-zag across the whole of Greek history, from Homer's *Odyssey* to the Nazi occupation, touching both the Peloponnesian War between ancient Athens and Sparta, and the Greek War of Independence from the Ottoman Turks. As things turned out, it included an excursion round the life and times of the de Villehardouin family from Champagne, who came to Greece with the Fourth Crusade in 1204 and controlled the Peloponnese for most of the thirteenth century.

For a long time I had had the notion to see the fortress of Chlemoutsi. This was built by Geoffrey II, the second of the Villehardouin princes of Achaea, between 1220 and 1230, to protect his capital at Andravida (which the Franks called Andreville) and its port of Clarence – Kyllini to Greeks both ancient and modern. My appetite was sharpened by the purchase of the Michelin guide to Greece in the French edition. This was not by choice, but because Likoudi's bookshop had no English copy in stock, but I never regretted it. It gave me a lot more than a pleasant sense of chic in reading Michelin in the original. The Greeks, on the whole, prefer to ignore the distasteful episode of the Latin Empire of Constantinople and the Frankish occupation of so much of their country. Their tourist literature makes little effort to steer the visitor in the direction of its crumbling remnants. But M. Michelin is not French for nothing. His guide dwells with affection and pride on this early flowering of French imperialism, and from the paragraphs headed 'Un peu d'histoire' it was possible to piece together a fair summary of the doings of a remarkable dynasty.

A LITTLE HISTORY

Geoffrey I of Achaea was the nephew of a high noble of Champagne, the Marshal William, one of the leaders of the Fourth Crusade, and also its chronicler. After the diversion of the crusade from its objectives in the Holy Land, and the shameful capture and sacking of Constantinople, the Byzantine lands in Greece were partitioned between the Venetians and the Franks. The Peloponnese, under the name of Achaea, fell to the lot of another Champenois lord, William of Champlitte, but by a mixture of luck and opportunism Geoffrey acquired his rights. He was recognised by the Latin Emperor Baldwin as the Prince, with many lesser barons as his vassals. He established his court at Andravida, inland from the port of Kyllini, which the French named

Clarence. He had other estates and residences in the Peloponnese, the principal ones being at Kalamata, in the southwest, and at Sparta, in the Eurotas valley. The latter was known as La Cremonie, a corruption of Lacedaemonia. (The French nobility appear to have been incapable of getting their tongues round Greek place names, almost all of which they mangled out of recognition.)

Geoffrey I died in 1218, leaving the reputation of an able, conciliatory ruler, popular with his subjects, both Franks and Greeks. His elder son Geoffrey succeeded him and maintained his father's tradition. His court is said to have rivalled, in wealth, fashion and the trappings of chivalry, anything that could be found in western Europe. Tourneys and courts of love were famous for their luxury and splendour. The prince maintained at his own expense eighty knights equipped with gilded spurs. The port became so rich that it was known as Clarence la Superbe. He built his great castle on an eminence, commanding the whole plain of Kyllini, and named it Clermont (later hellenised as Chlemoutsi). Here he was permitted to establish a mint and to issue his own gold coinage. This bore the image of the façade of the church of St Martin at Tours, and the pieces were known as Tournois. (From this, Clermont became known as Château Tournois, later Italianised as Castel Tornese.) His reign was the zenith of Frankish ascendancy in Greece. Geoffrey died in 1246, without heirs of the body, and was succeeded by his brother William.

William de Villehardouin was as forceful a character as his older brother. An inveterate and aggressive warrior, he was determined to consolidate his control of the Peloponnese. He built two more major castles, one on a strong-point above the Eurotas valley, to protect his Lacedaemonian court from the marauding Slavs of Taygetus. He called this Mizithra, or Mistra. The second was La Maina in the Mani, to keep the local inhabitants in order. William also attacked the surviving Byzantine stronghold of Monemvasia on the east coast, which the Franks knew as Malvoisie (transmuted by the English, who enjoyed its wine, into Malmsey). The siege lasted for three years, by the end of which the citizens, 'shut up like nightin-gales in a cage', were reduced to eating cats and mice and were allowed to surrender with honour.

It is difficult not to be fond of William. He was a big, fair-haired man with prominent front teeth, but felt more Greek than he looked. Born at Kalamata, he spoke Greek as his first language, and loved the country and its people. They returned his affection, and considered that he ruled as justly as any Byzantine despot would have done. He also had the good sense to marry a Greek girl. He had been twice widowed and had no children. She was Anna, one of the two beautiful daughters of the Despot of Epiros, Michael Angelos, bastard of a former imperial family and a pretender to the throne of Constantinople. The marriage took place at Arta, the Angelos capital. It was a promising dynastic alliance, but did William no practical good in the end.

Almost at once, Michael sent for his son-in-law to help him in resisting an invasion by the forces of the rival Nicaean pretender. William rode north with all his lords and the feudal levies of his principality, to form part of the Epirot army. Battle was finally joined on the plain of Pelagonia, in Western Macedonia (where 1,500 years before the Spar-tan Brasidas, scourge of the Athenians, with 3,000 Hellenic hoplites, defeated the Illyrians). Michael the Despot's army was routed. William tried to escape, in civilian dress, but was discovered hiding under a heap of straw and recognised by his tell-tale teeth. He was taken to Nicaea and imprisoned. The ransom demanded was the surrender of the castles at Monem-vasia, Mistra and Maina. For three years this was resolutely refused, but eventually a feudal council was held at Nikli, composed of so many wives and widows of barons that it was known as the Parliament of Ladies. Unsurprisingly the women thought it more important to make love than war. The castles were handed over, and William was restored to his marriage bed.

Frankish power was permanently weakened, but William and Anne's marriage was happy and successful, except that they produced no male heir, only two daughters. William died in 1278, at Kalamata his birthplace, and was buried in the church of the Knights Templar at Andravida. The de Villehardouin story was done.

English history added a postscript. Edward III's queen, Philippa of Hainault, was descended from one of the de Villehardouin daughters, and brought with her into the royal family the title of the Duchy of Clarence. When Shakespeare's 'false, fleeting, perjur'd Clarence' was dispatched, at Richard III's command, in a malmsey-butt, Monemvasia had some sort of revenge.

AROUND KYLLINI

The *Phaedra* deposited us on the quayside at Patras in the cold dawn. With luggage for a week and no transport, we grew increasingly irritable on the pavements till a miraculous café burst into life and produced the tourist's panacea, a Full English Breakfast. Within an hour, stowed in a roomy hired Nissan, with full hearts and stomachs, we were on the National Highway to Pyrgos, the town of Olympia.

Half persuaded that Chlemoutsi might prove worth the detour, Patrick turned off into the Kyllini peninsula, in the north-west corner of the Peloponnese. Some way short of the port we noticed a mention in Michelin of an old convent, dedicated to the Virgin of Vlachernai, 'qui se dissimule dans un vallon solitaire et verdoyant'. The vision of a self-dissimulating nunnery was so compelling that, at Kato Panayia (nether All-holy-Lady), we made a detour within a detour, and found the secluded object of our quest, exactly as described.

As we approached the entrance, a strange, thin, middle-aged woman came running towards us down the slope outside the perimeter wall, and offered to be our guide, without payment. She spoke fair English, distorted by the fact that she was totally toothless. She explained that her teeth had fallen out after electric shock treatment for a mental breakdown, which had ended both her marriage and an academic career. We learned from her that the convent had finally run out of nuns nine years before. The local bishop decided to use it as a refuge for physically and mentally handicapped men and women. Now there were twenty in residence, with a small nursing staff, under the direction of an archimandrite.

Our guide showed us the *katholikon*, the convent church. This was a Byzantine building of great age, to which Cistercian monks of the Frankish occupation had made Gothic additions. The resulting lop-sided mongrel was an architectural curiosity rather than a thing of beauty, and has also suffered serious structural damage in recent earthquakes. But it had fine floor tiles and, on the templon, an icon of the Virgin Odhiyitria, of serious and disturbing beauty.

We were joined in the church by one of the nurses, a young woman married to an air force officer, who took us to meet the director. The large court was shaded by orange trees and bejewelled with peacocks, in an old monastic tradition which held the birds to symbolise the Resurrection. Inmates sat about under the trees, or passed slowly on real or imagined errands. In a big upper room the director, a pleasant young monk, entertained us over cups of Greek coffee. A silent girl with a troubled face attached herself to our company and sat constantly adjusting the shoulders of her blouse, but was not reproved or sent away. At the far end of the room, in front of a stuffed peacock and two adjacent television sets, a barber was shaving a dwarf's face. A notice pinned to the wall set out, hour by hour, the innocent routine of the day. We made a donation, took photographs of our companions, and left filled with a sense of tranquillity, healing and goodness.

Our road avoided both Kyllini and Andravida and took us across the fertile, sunlit plain directly to Chlemoutsi. Here the level land swells to a circular hill, at the top of which, out of purple and gold banks of mallow and marigold, the sheer dark walls of the fortress sprang, as if cast up by eruption. They were double, of such massive construction as to contain within their width halls and even a chapel. Time had made little impression on their solidity, but on passing through the tunnel of the gateway we found that little was left of the inner courts, and the chambers of French dalliance. The worn grey stones of the stairways were picked out in splashes of red poppy. Apart from some workmen carrying out restoration, we were the only people there. We mounted to the top of the ramparts. The only sentinels were crows, and a jackdaw wearing a gold cross on a chain round its neck. Beyond Elis, the blue Ionian stretched to a gilded cloud which was Zakynthos – Isola Zante, Fior del Levante.

On the wall outside the great gate, the town of Kyllini has affixed a plaque, recording, with proper patriotism, the fact that in 1429 the castle became Greek, when it was taken by Constantine Palaiologos, later to be the last Emperor of Byzantium. We had had enough history for one day and headed for the seaside, only stopping on the way, in a grove of giant poplars hung with creepers, to drink a celebratory ouzo from our reserve fuel stock. At Loutra Kyllinis the sea lapped lazily on a long empty beach of pale fine sand, fringed by pine-clad dunes, and we swam in the shallows and ate our lunch under the trees, to the chatter of a charm of goldfinches.

PYRGOS TO VATHEIA

We shared the hotel at Pyrgos with a coachload of middle-aged Californians. Undersized and overweight, arrayed in a medley of outfits of bizarre cuts and colours, and calling to each other in impenetrable San Diegan, they seemed as improbable as visitors from Outer Space. The town was almost entirely given over to supplying aliens' needs, but we found ouzo in a café occupied, more or less, by a hairy rural papas and his extended family, and from there were directed to a small restaurant where an agreeable girl cooked proper food for us.

Early morning Olympia was almost as quiet as Marily and I remembered it from our visit with Susan and Archie twenty-five years before, the most undemanding, almost soothing, of all the major ancient sites. This may be because Poseidon the Earth-Shaker has left scarcely a stone standing, so that there are no wonders of the world to admire. There had been one change, and that for the better. The new museum provided a far nobler setting for old favourites – the Hermes, Pheidias's cup, Miltiades' helmet – while the sculptures from the pediment of Zeus's temple had been arranged in their correct relationship to each other. The classical creativeness, craftsmanship and sure sense of beauty have never been surpassed.

Kyparissia, on the coast between Pyrgos and Pylos, was another personal fief of William de Villehardouin, at that time called Arkadia. We stopped there, not for that reason, but because Lily Condi had recommended that we should eat lunch at Nynio's. The restaurant, run by Dionysus and his son Achilleas, was an old-style eating-house, a square room decorated with black-and-white photographs of family ancestors, oil cloth on the tables, and straight-up-and-down wooden chairs with cane seats. The place was fully of hearty men, who could have been the town council off duty, or members of the local hunters' association. Mention of Lily's name produced immediate ouzo and *mezedhes* all round. A fish lunch of grilled *sphyrida* cost us roughly half of what we had expected to pay. Dionysus accepted our congratulations with the depressing information that next year he would be serving fast food, as the only thing that pays these days.

Pylos was doggedly undistinguished. Homer's sandy Pylos; Pylos, on whose island of Spachteria the Athenians won their surprise victory over the Spartans; Pylos, Port des Joncs to the Franks, and Navarino to the Byzantines, where Codrington blew the Turkish fleet out of the water and assured Greek independence; Pylos now was a small, nineteenth-century harbour town, with a civic statute of its hero – Kostis Tsikitiras, who won the long jump gold medal at the 1912 Olympics, and died of meningitis on army service. The view from our balcony of the harbour and its craft was as photogenic at dawn as at dusk. The hotel itself was mediocre, the waterfront food unworthy of its ambience, while the only source of recreation appeared to be the quay where contemplative anglers dangled bait in opaque water. A pair of these, elderly men, fished all night below the hotel. They came, they told us, from different towns but had met at Pylos regularly for many years, for their annual fishing trip.

If Pylos had disappointed, Methoni, a few miles to the south, gave unexpected delight. Called by the Venetians Modon, it, with nearby Koroni, was the only part of the Peloponnese which they kept in their own possession after 1204. They retained it continuously until its capture by the Turks in 1500. A strong fort was erected on the promontory, and it became a rich and important post on the Venetian trade route to Crete and the Middle East. We saw it on a calm idyllic morning. The cincture of the walls, reaching out to sea from a sand-gold bay, is still intact, ending in a massive sea-gate and a causeway to an islet crowned by a round toy Turkish tower. Within, nothing remains of the fort but fallen walls, half buried in yellow horned poppies, capers and verbascum, where white butterflies sipped and flitted. The only intact building was a Church of the Transfiguration, of later construction, still apparently in use, but with an unglazed circular window through which swallows and martins were flying to their nests, respectively along the walls and in the corners of the interior.

We bought a picnic, with ouzo, in the village and retraced our way through Pylos to Nestor's palace in the hills. The remains seemed about the size of a largish country house, and the main hall with its round central hearth no bigger than an ordinary living-room. But the location fits well enough with the Odyssey description of the kingdom of old Nestor. Perhaps a young man called Telemachus did really come here for news of his father, and was feasted on Pylos beach, and brought to the palace to sit by the hearth and listen to the verbose old hero's tales of bygone days. Certainly the handsome stone bath looked like a queen's. As at Methoni, we were the only visitors. We chatted with the custodian, who kept a garden bright with pansies and was worried by the lack of rain.

So we set our faces for the Mani. In a gentle valley above Kalamata we ate our picnic by the stream bed, and a passing police car tooted 'good appetite'. Then on by the scenic coastal road past Kardamyli - home to Patrick Leigh Fermor – into ever more rugged country till we came at evening to Vatheia.

DEEPEST MANI

Outwardly, Vatheia must have looked much the same as we saw it when Leigh Fermor came for the first time, not long after the war, led to hospitality by the girl Vasilio, who carried a lamb slung across her shoulders. As in many Maniot villages, a high proportion of the houses are tall square towers, giving the place the look of a miniature San Gimignano. These were the result of rivalry and jealousy between the leading families, who constantly tried to out-build each other. More specifically, when a feud exploded into open warfare, extra height enabled one to bombard an enemy's marble roof with boulders.

The number and size of the towers give an idea of the population and, within the resources of the region, the prosperity of the Mani until fairly recent times. So, too, does the intense terracing of the stony hillsides. These must have yielded crops, as well as the surviving olive trees stunted but the shallowness of soil. Now the terraces grow only wild oats. Vatheia itself was practically deserted, but in 1821 the Maniot chief, Petrobey Mavromichalis, was able to lead a private army of 3,000 men to capture Kalamata from the Turks and proclaim himself prince.

The Greek Tourist Board had rented two of the towers,

and converted the lower floors into a *xenonas*, or guest house. The rooms were entirely of stone, but clean and comfortable enough, with hot water. A restaurant provided adequate food, cooked by Kyria Eleni, who owned a tower in the village but lived in Athens during the winter. The manager lived close by with his wife and three children. The wife, Areti (which means Virtue), was very dark, with thick jet-black locks and something of a moustache. She was gentler than her looks, and took Marily and me to see the little church (dedicated, surprisingly, to our own St Spyridon) which she obviously tended with devotion.

On our first day Patrick and Mary took the car to Mistra, which they had not seen before. While Marily painted, I explored the village and met with an English trio, two ladies and a gentleman of respectable mien. They had sensible shoes and rucksacks, and informed me that they had walked up from the fishing village of Yerolimani, where they were on a wild flower holiday, organised by the Ramblers' Association. They were much taken by the cotton-thistles with strikingly large purple flowers, and were amused to learn that their name, since classical times, means a donkey's fart. As we parted, the man said that he had at first wondered if I might perhaps be Mr Leigh Fermor, which I took as a compliment.

The weather had turned unsettled. Taygetos held a dark threat of rain, and was spilling mist over the tops of its ridges to veil the sun from us. Once this had lifted, the warmth began to spice the air with scent of lavender, thyme, throumbi and summer savoury. The dominant plant was spurge, in bushes like giant pincushions, green, pink, coral and scarlet, growing so close together that from a distance a hillside would seem to be covered in patchwork. The fragrance of herbs persisted all day, everywhere. In the afternoon Marily and I walked above the village to its cemetery. The family tombs were stark cubes of cement, between six and ten feet high, like a grisly Maniot town for dead midgets. From across the valley two ravens ominously cronked.

Patrick and Mary returned very wet. At the highest point of
the castle at Mistra the Taygetos cloud had burst, catching
them at the maximum distance from the car. Notorious cour-
tiers of discomfort, they were unmoved, and soon ready to
go out to supper. The taverna on the shore at Yerolimenas
was full – if appearances did not lie – of brigands and pirates,
watching basketball on television. Only when the match was
over did they sit down, at a long table, to a supper which had
involved cooking about 200 quails, almost certainly illegally
hunted at that time of year.

Early the following morning a little owl was calling, and
at breakfast time it was sitting on a corner of our tower,
Athena's bird, holding in its beak by the tail a twitching,
foot-long snake. With this augury, we set off southwards,
beyond Vatheia, stopping first for coffee at Porto Caio, a bay
with a tiny hamlet which takes its name from *quaglio*, Italian
for quail. This is the last stop for European quails on their
autumn migration, before making the sea crossing to Africa.
In the old days, the birds were netted here in their thousands,
and were exported to the kitchens of Italy and France. Fishermen had just landed a catch of small fish and were still
detaching the last of them from their net. We ordered some for
our luch and headed off for Cape Tainaron and the gate of
Hades. The landscape became more and more infernal, and we
eventually gave up and swam at the grey sand beach of
Marmari, before going back for a long lazy munching, loung-
ing and sketching afternoon at Porto Caio. We saw shrikes,
several cirl buntings, and one Cretschmar's.

SOUTH TO NORTH

We left early for Monemvasia. On the day before, above
Porto Caio, there had been a lone tower, with a large crown
painted on it in green, symbol of the Greek monarchy. At the
time of the civil war, when the return of King George II
from exile was a fierce issue, this had been a common sight,

but I had not seen it on a wall for at least twenty years. That the Mani still kept something of its traditional monarchist allegiance emerged again when we halted to buy local honey at Pirgos Dirou. Learning that Patrick was on his way to England, the beekeeper asked him to bear greetings to 'my king' and, fishing out a wallet from next to his heart, produced a small photograph of the exiled King Constantine.

From Pirgos Dirou it is possible to see the remains of William de V.'s castle of La Maina, on the Tigani headland. By making the detour to Monemvasia on the way to Sparta we thus traced the triangle of William's ransom.

Monemvasia was worth the detour, if only as a curiosity. With its houses clinging like barnacles to the precipitous sides of a huge rock, almost completely surrounded by the sea, it must have been virtually impregnable. The length of the siege is not surprising. Architecturally, however, it was unremarkable, and the town had the dead feel of a place uninhabited except by those making a living from tourists. Little is left of the *castro* at the summit, to which we toiled in considerable heat, but there was at least one of the finest views in Greece, and a solid medieval church of the Holy Wisdom, shaded by an olive of incalculable age, and set among purple hollyhocks.

We picnicked in a wood near the shore and drove straight to Sparta. The Menelaion hotel was old-fashioned and sensible, with big baths, and charged £25 per bed and breakfast, for two. They recommended a taverna, at which the helpings were so large that we kept half the meat for the next day's picnic.

Our road ran through Arcady, in the heart of the Peloponnese. Green pastures and woods, and at one part purple carpets of lavender under the olives. At Mantineia, Michelin did us a last favour by pointing us to a disconcerting modern church, dedicated to the Blessed Virgin, Beethoven, and the Nine Muses, designed by a Greek-American architect, in every known style and from every possible different material.

Then up and over into the upper valley of the Vodaiko –
where the walnut groves had been blackened and withered by
some plague – and down to Kalavryta. This was a sort of goal
of pilgrimage for Marily, for it was here on 25 March 1821
that Archbishop Germanos first raised the banner of revolt
against the Ottoman oppressors, and set the War of Independence alight. The banner, the Lavaron, along with others relics,
is kept at the monastery of Ayia Lavra, outside the town. If
cleanliness is next to godliness, the monastery is as far from
God as the nunnery of Vlachernae is near Him. The monks
were dirty, mercenary and unfriendly, while the car-park
lavatories were the filthiest in my experience.

A signpost directs one from the town to the spot where, in
the last war, the Germans took every adult male in Kalavryta and shot them dead, in reprisal for hostile acts of resistance. There is also the terminus of an unusual railway line, on
which a rack-and-pinion locomotive hauls small carriages up
the Vodaiko gorge from Diakofto on the Gulf of Corinth.
Patrick expressed an urge, either alone or in company, to use
this means of travel, but the timetable did not suit. So, pausing only to buy rose-petal jam at Mega Spileon, we began
the giddy, 3,000-foot descent by road. At Ano Diakofto the
cherry orchards were hung, like a child's painting, with glowing fruit. When we stopped to buy cherries from an old couple
sitting at the roadside, they invited us to sit on their bench and
refresh ourselves with glasses of cold water. We bought the
cherries of Paradise, and they gave us three lemons as a present.
So with the taste of the Peloponnese in our mouths and hearts
we came to the sea, Patras, the El Greco, and home.

Epilogue: Sunday, 28 October 1990

When we are staying in the village we attend Sunday service at the church as a matter of course. It cannot be said that we do so with much regularity or religious fervour – the Greek Orthodox do not harp tiresomely on those themes – but we feel obliged to show solidarity, both with Father Spiro who (even if he does little else) has to perform his priestly function every Lord's Day and deserves some sort of congregation, and also with the diminishing band of the faithful from the old days. There is also the matter of keeping on the right side of Irene. She discourages spiritual laxity and tries to keep our souls as spotless as our floors. She also is hurt if we do not sometimes compliment her on her rendering of the hymns which, on weekdays, she practises in our garlic-fragrant kitchen.

Various reasons, some more convincing than others, had reduced attendance during the summer, and conscience goaded me to put in an appearance on our last day before shutting Kapoutsi for the winter. Marily pleaded frailty and domestic business, so I went alone. The long drought had broken. The night had been pyrotechnical with a continuous old-fashioned Corfu thunderstorm, and it was still raining heavily. The garden smelt sweetly of wet earth, with a whiff of anise, as if Ganymede had spilled the ouzo on Olympus. I parked the car near Hector the baker's. The village seemed deserted, but a clamour of bells broke out below me, where the church of the Odyiyitria looks out across the valley to the mountain of the Ten Saints. I picked my way gingerly down the dripping flagstones of the steep lane, water spouting and gushing across my path from gutters and runnels, and scurried gratefully into the shelter of the porch and an unusually powerful sound of singing.

I knew, of course, that it was a Greek National Day, second only to the Epanastasis celebrations on 25 March, with parades of dignitaries and soldiers and schoolchildren in every town, led by brass bands. Somehow, I had not expected anything very special in a village church. Clearly, however, this was to be no ordinary Liturgy. Bay leaves had been scattered over the black and white tiling of the floor; in front of the All-Holy Virgin's icon a cross had been set, flanked by two tall candlesticks hung with black ribbon; Irene and the octogenarian Gerasimos had been augmented by two extra psaltes from the village and a young man, new to me, of magnificent lung-power, as well as our friend Spiro 'Mantou' who has a horrible voice, but is indispensable as master of ceremonies on formal village occasions; and old Vasili our neighbour was wearing his best dark suit, and a tie. Under-dressed, but reluctant to go home and change, I lit my candles and niched myself in one of the wooden stalls along the south wall.

Harmoniously, deliberately, a doxology wound its way along. Little by little, one became aware of a competing twitter, as though a flock of chaffinches were gathering in the back narthex, and eventually its source erupted into church in the shape of about forty primary school children, who were then herded forward, directly in front of me, by their *daskalos*, the village dominie. They all looked extremely clean, their dark heads shone from assiduous brushing, they all wore their best uniform – white shirts for boys, white blouses and dark blue skirts for girls, and they maintained a constant and irrepressible turmoil of good-humoured chatter, teasing, waving to friends, and putting bay leaves on each other's heads, which provided a fringe entertainment to the Divine Liturgy. The children were shortly followed by a contingent of the younger members of the village *mousiki* – a *'bandina'* – half a dozen girl clarinettists and boys on brass and big drum. Led by the little bandmaster (old Vasili's successor) they took up position in the middle of the nave, in their navy blue uniforms with crimson piping, and with crimson-plumed brass helmets under their right arms. A few – very few – parents came to keep an eye on their offspring. The village president, Taki, joined the official party opposite the choir, and was joined, finally, by old Papa Pipi, our retired priest, in his very best blacks, complete with cylindrical hat and black umbrella.

Meanwhile the current Papa Spiro's gentle voice flowed on, in Byzantine measure, from behind the iconostasis. Twice it was interrupted to allow the musicians to put on their helmets and play, with accuracy and feeling, a piece of solemn melody (mimicked, naturally, by several ten-year-old humorists). At the close of the service they executed a jolly march tune, and we moved - about an hour and a half from the start of the whole performance – into an extension devoted to patriotic commemoration. Prayers from the fallen were sung. Irene delivered her *pièce de résistance*, the embellished version of the Trisagion. The president laid a wreath at the foot of the cross, and a small boy and girl each did likewise. The assistant schoolmaster then read out his hand-written account of the events of 1940, of Mussolini's arrogant ultimatum, of Metaxas' historic 'No', of the halting of the Italian invasion and the heroic defence of the snow-covered mountain frontier, through that winter when nowhere else in Europe was there resistance to Axis aggression. 'Zito i Ellada. May Greece live.' he ended. 'Zito,' replied the congregation, and remembering that dark Christmas of fifty years ago, 'Zito,' I said.

The *bandina* put on their helmets for the last time, and we stood as they played the national anthem of Greece, the Hymn of Liberty. Emotion pricked my eyes. 'O my people,' I said silently, 'though you may not know it, you are part of me.'